Items should be return   before the last date shown
below.
tele

Jim Kemmy

About the Author

Brian Callanan is a planner in the Limerick Region and is particularly interested in the history of the area. In 2000 he published *Ireland's Shannon Story*.

JIM KEMMY

Stonemason, Trade Unionist, Politician, Historian

Brian Callanan

The Liffey Press

Published by
The Liffey Press
Ashbrook House, 10 Main Street
Raheny, Dublin 5, Ireland
www.theliffeypress.com

A catalogue record of this book is
available from the British Library.

ISBN 978-1-908308-07-8

Printed in Spain by GraphyCems.

Contents

Preface

Jim Kemmy's life was all of a piece. Stonemason and socialist, trade unionist and political activist, writer and historian, parliamentarian and humanist. Jim Kemmy was, by any standards a big man, big in heart and big in frame, he was a towering presence in the life of Limerick for more than three decades, and to many others elsewhere in Ireland and beyond.

So spoke Professor Gearóid Ó Tuathaigh of NUI Galway at the funeral oration for Kemmy in 1997. Following Ó Tuathaigh's vision of the man, this book explores the life of Jim Kemmy, profiling the different 'pieces' of his life during those years. The story of Kemmy's life is worth telling, not only because it is the history of one significant person, but also because it reflects issues of an entire society, viewed through the eyes of one of its activists. Kemmy's life spans a period of immense transformation in Irish society with controversy and change in so many aspects – Northern Ireland, family planning, industrial relations, religious beliefs, the Labour Party, local government, heritage and environment, to name but some of the main issues that engaged him. The life of Jim Kemmy echoes those controversies. The book is also significant in that it is a review of a local activist, and, in his own language, a working-class one. So often, biographies are dominated by the 'big players' with substantial national or international profiles. But the local actors have their stories to tell too, often stories that illuminate magnificently the forces of change in society, and stories of people who helped shape their country's future. Jim Kemmy's is such a story.

The idea of a biography of Jim Kemmy was suggested by his friend, Patsy Harrold, during a social evening with my wife, Sheila and our friends Bríd Hayes and Gay Kilgarriff.

This work has drawn on the support and help of several people. Joe Kemmy, Jim's brother, provided encouragement, advice and information. The Special Collections Unit at the Library of the University of Limerick made available a wealth of documentation on the different aspects of Jim Kemmy's life: heartiest thanks to Ken Bergin, Siobhan Morrisey and Jean Turner. Anna-Maria Hajba was the archivist who compiled the Kemmy Collection, also giving valuable advice to the author. Mike Allen, general secretary of the Labour Party, provided additional material. Adrian Butler of the *Limerick Leader* provided photographs. Mike McGuire of Limerick City Library provided access to the archives of the *Limerick Leader*. Interviews were given by Niall Greene (Labour Party), Brendan Halligan (then editor of the *Limerick Leader*), Seamus Harrold (activist), Ray Kavanagh (then general secretary of the Labour Party), Dan Miller (Labour Party and trade unionist), Foncie McCoy (trade unionist), Mike McNamara (Building and Allied Trades Union (BATU)), Joe O'Brien (Construction Industry Federation), Margaret O'Donoghue (secretary to Jim Kemmy), Manus O'Riordan (trade unionist) Jan O'Sullivan, TD, Pat Reeves (trade unionist), Dick Spring (then leader of the Labour Party) and Joe Wallace (University of Limerick).

Thanks to the family team for their love and support: Sheila, Jill, Hilary and Ronan.

Any errors or omissions are entirely the responsibility of the author.

Brian Callanan
Limerick
July 2011

Foreword

Jim Kemmy's death in late September 1997 was marked by an extraordinary sense of public loss and a show of public affection unusual in Irish political life. He had never held high office in the state or government. In fact, in national politics he had been a combative and regularly controversial voice on a number of major, bitterly-contested and divisive issues within the Irish body politic for most of the previous three decades – church-state relations, Northern Ireland and the 'national question', the role of the state in achieving a balance between individual liberties and the 'common good'. Indeed, even his relationship with the leadership of the party of which he eventually became the proud and highly-regarded Chairman in 1992 – the Labour Party – had been troubled and testy for long interludes during the previous twenty years. He had been one of those political figures who stir things up in public debate. Yet the general response to his passing was almost entirely free of recrimination.

The fact that by the later 1990s a measure of consensus had been reached – or was emerging – on several of the most seismically divisive issues that had marked his public career of advocacy can only partially explain the almost universal expressions of respect, across the political spectrum, that marked his passing. Nor can one simply record, as an explanation, that he himself had mellowed and had reached accommodations of tolerance with one-time foes and adversaries, while holding to his own views firmly and with integrity. Changed circumstances, the natural exhaustion of seemingly volcanic enmities, and, globally, the need for the 'Left' to regroup and reassess a future for popularly-supported social democracy, in the wake of the collapse of the Soviet empire and system and the seemingly invincible triumph of market-driven liberal capitalism (championed by the Reagan-Thatcher axis): all of these factors are clearly relevant to the political space occupied by Jim Kemmy at the time of his death. Nor should one neglect the glow of legend that surrounded him: 'the man who brought down a government because of its attempt to put a tax on children's shoes'.

Beyond all of these factors, however, the ultimate explanation of why Jim Kemmy's early death was so widely mourned probably lies in the inscrutable domain of 'character'. Jim Kemmy had a flinty integrity, an open, uncalculating honesty of purpose and manner, and a humane instinct that people recognized as utterly wholesome and to which the better part of their own nature responded warmly. By dint of reading, reflection, and the deeper understanding that comes from life experience, he worked his way through difficult public issues and controversies. On national issues, trade union disputes and negotiations, or local contentions, not all were persuaded that he always got it right. But nobody doubted his over-riding commitment to fairness and justice for those who had trouble securing either, or to his general declaration that 'ideology should serve the people' rather than the other way around.

No great toil of analysis or explanation is needed to account for the universal sense of loss and affection, which marked Jim Kemmy's passing, in Limerick, his native city. He had come to 'embody' the spirit of the city, not only through his service in public office (including two terms as Mayor), but by his ubiquitous and generous presence at the heart of all that was progressive and elevating in civic renewal, respect for heritage and the celebration of local history, over several decades. His most notable publications – the *Old Limerick Journal*, the *Limerick Anthology* and the *Limerick Compendium* – gave a sense of pride to all citizens of Limerick, whatever their creed or politics. Likewise, those bodies and civic groups charged with the maintenance of the physical fabric of the city, its public buildings and cultural institutions, all found in Jim Kemmy a steadfast and generous supporter. One would like to think that it must have been some small solace to him, in his last days, to know that his lifetime of service to Limerick and its people was fully acknowledged and deeply appreciated.

The story of the earnest young man who returned to Limerick in 1960, after three years in England as an emigrant stonemason, highly politicized and determined to make his mark and to bring about change in his native country, is a story well worth the telling. Kemmy's story illumines many important themes and episodes in the recent history of Ireland. It also recalls a man who was unstinting in his efforts to make that Ireland a better place for all its citizens, but especially for those whose honest labour creates its wealth and whose cause needs to be championed, in good times and bad, in order for them to claim their due.

Gearóid Ó Tuathaigh
Professor Emeritus in History,
NUI,Galway
July 2011

Chronology

1936	Jim Kemmy born in Limerick to Michael and Elizabeth Kemmy
1957	Emigrates to London, working as stonemason
1960	Returns to Limerick working in Shannon industrial estate; joins the Labour Party
	Branch secretary of Limerick Stonemasons union
1965	Starts working in Limerick City Council as stonemason
	Becomes secretary of the Limerick Building Trades Group
	Becomes chairman of Limerick Trades Council
1972	Resigns from the Labour Party
	First edition of the *Limerick Socialist*
1974	Elected as councillor to Limerick City Council

1974	Leads establishment of family planning clinic in Limerick
	President of Limerick Mechanics' Institute
1978	First edition of the *Old Limerick Journal*
1981	Elected to the Dáil
	Leaves employment in Limerick City Council to concentrate on political/trade union work
1982	Causes the collapse of the first Fitzgerald coalition government
	Loses his Dáil seat in November
	Formation of Democratic Socialist Party
1987	Re-elected to Dáil
1990	Re-joins Labour Party
1991	Mayor of Limerick
1992	Becomes chairman of the Labour Party
1995	Mayor of Limerick
1996	Publication of the *Limerick Anthology*
1997	Publication of *Limerick from Old Postcards*
	Death of Jim Kemmy
1998	Publication (posthumously) of the *Limerick Compendium*

1

Early Years

The Ireland of the mid-twentieth century followed a period of new beginnings and developments: war of independence, civil war, the new state – the fledgling governments with new policies, such as electricity generation in the 1920s and protection of native industry in the 1930s. All around were social and economic changes: the international depression and emigration, with rural decline and the weakening of traditional life-styles, combined with the incipient beginnings of urbanisation and the slow growth of fresh ideas. It is in this context that the Jim Kemmy story has its roots.

Born on 14 September 1936, Kemmy's political philosophy was shaped by all these factors, as well as his local setting and family heritage. Activism was in his blood, and owed its origins to previous generations of his family. His grandfather, Joseph Kemmy, had been a stonemason and visited Russia in the 1890s, one of a group of Limerick stonemasons and pork butchers providing technical advice to Russian workers in the construction and food industries. In those days, there were important reasons why the Russian industrialists would look to Limerick for support and help. Limerick was a centre of the bacon industry, an industry dependent on the firing of kilns.

These kilns had to be lined with brick, hence the importance of stonemasons. Kemmy's grandfather had lined the kilns in Shaw's bacon factory in Limerick. Requests for help from Russian companies for technical support in lining their kilns resulted in a group of Limerick bacon curers and stonemasons being sent to train the Russian workers in the bacon industry. In an article on Limerick's stonemasons in 1963, the *Limerick Leader* noted this event:[1]

> A tribute to the craftsmanship (of Limerick stonemasons) was paid by Russian industrialists in 1890 when six Limerick masons, experts in the lining of furnace boilers with firebrick, travelled with technicians from one of our local bacon factories to start the bacon-curing industry in Russia. Russian bricklayers could not compete with Limerick's skills in the lining of boilers.

Joseph Kemmy, one of this group, was a recognised expert stonemason in fireclay and furnace work and helped in the building of St John's Cathedral in Limerick.

Following this tradition, Jim Kemmy's father, Michael Kemmy, was also a stonemason. In addition he was reported to be an enthusiastic reader with a love for literature, a sculptor and painter in his free time, described by friends as a 'gentleman who loved poetry and philosophy'. But the wider extended family also exerted an influence. A neighbour, Pat Reeves, explained: 'Apart from his father and grandfather, Jim also had two uncles living in Limerick, both were stonemasons, so the stonemason tradition was in his veins, he was rooted in the stonemasons.'

Jim Kemmy's mother was Elizabeth Pilkington from Kilmihil in County Clare, one of fourteen children (thirteen of whom emigrated to America), who met his father after coming to work in a shop in Limerick. She too brought a love of books, and also a spirit of self-reliance, growing her own vegetables in her back garden. Trade unionist Dan Miller told the author: 'Jim epitomised the impact of strong values, these he certainly got from his home environment, through his mother and father, and he experienced other influences later on the building sites in Britain.'

Originally living in O'Curry Street, the family moved to Garryowen soon after Jim Kemmy's birth.[2] Pat Reeves reported that the Kemmy family moved into a privately-owned house, a two-story family home on a half-acre, one of three properties owned by his family. 'The Kemmys were definitely not poor,' said Pat Reeves. Garryowen at the time would have been an old community, but also the location for a relatively new development, one of the new Corporation housing estates built at the time to relieve the poor housing conditions in the centre of the city. The house into which they moved had been a family home for several generations, the Kemmys having lived in Garryowen for 150 years, according to Kemmy himself.[3] This experience of multi-generational living in one community, over several decades, would have had substantial consequences for Jim Kemmy. In terms of his own perceptions, this tradition emotionally rooted him in the area, bestowing an enthusiasm and passion for the history and heritage for the community, one that was to grow on him over the years ahead. In terms of other people, his roots gave Kemmy access to links and networks throughout the city, locating Kemmy within a wide system of extended family that grew out of his kindred relations spanning the city. This fact would have obvious ramifications for Kemmy's local political strengths, enlarging his sphere of influence through personal contacts, familial bonds and social connections.

The Limerick of the 1930s and 1940s, as Jim Kemmy grew up, was a substantial industrial town, with significant companies in food processing (particularly bacon curing), shoes and clothing manufacture. Owned by Irish merchant families, with origins stretching back to the nineteenth century, these companies were supported by Irish government policies of the time, providing heavy protection for Irish manufacturers against competing imports, with restrictions on inward investment in favour of domestic industry. Limerick's port location was a further stimulus to its industrial character, a point for import and export of trade. With that type of economic profile, issues of worker/management relationships, with their associated challenges of trade union/employer interaction, were never far from the surface. Compounding this were the problems of unemployment and emigration, with 50,000 people emigrating from Ireland annually by the 1950s.

Many of these tensions were illustrated by Frank McCourt's award-winning book *Angela's Ashes* (1996), a memoir of growing up in Limerick in the 1930s and 1940s, with an alcoholic father, struggling mother, impoverished family and fear of eternal damnation brought on by religion – a rich story delivered through biting satire, reflecting the inner conflicts of the social class divisions of an Irish town, with McCourt particularly targeting the church, property owners and charity-givers. The social tensions inherent in this context would have provided fertile ground for Jim Kemmy's thinking.

Joe Kemmy explained some of the family influences. His father, Michael Kemmy, was a strong sketcher and painter, also enjoying sculpture from working small figures from metal moulds.

> He worked in CIE as a stonemason on the bridges along the railway lines. He would be away a lot up the country. In theory he would be required to stay away at work, but often managed to sneak a lift home on one of the railway carriages, slipping away early on a train the following morning.

Joe recalls him bringing home plants and cuttings from the countryside.

Their mother, with rural roots, was an active gardener. They had a large garden set with cabbage, onions, geese and hens. 'From Clare, she had all the skills, building a dry wall, a most resourceful woman,' said Joe Kemmy. These resources would undoubtedly have flowed from Elizabeth Kemmy's own background as one of 14 children in a west Clare labouring family, encompassing all the ingredients for imaginative self-reliance.

Jim Kemmy had four immediate siblings. His brother Michael was a strong soccer player, captaining the Irish Youth team, became a stonemason and emigrated to the US, but tragically died from illness at the relatively young age of 34. Joan (Hartnett), living in Limerick, developed strong interests in local history. Maureen (McAteer), living in Donegal, became an accomplished poet. Joe, living in Limerick, was a bricklayer and worked as a strong partner of Jim Kemmy throughout his political career. Joe Kemmy told the author that the family have a half-brother, P.J. Pilkington, a child of their mother from an earlier relationship. This would suggest that Elizabeth Pilkington was a single mother at the time of her wedding, with her first child being nurtured by her extended family of origin. That this fact had been no barrier to a happy marriage in the Limerick and Clare of the 1930s, given the taboos of the time, amply illustrates the versatility of the Kemmy and Pilkington families. A further member, Mary Troy, joined the Kemmy family at a later date, as a foster child, yet again illustrating the family's open resilience. So the domestic background from whence Kemmy originated provided a substantial foundation for the confidence and imagination that he would later display.

In primary school in Limerick, Jim Kemmy showed early potential, winning a scholarship in Irish, and also a medal in *Féile Luimní*, a local schools drama competition. One teacher remarked that his essays were excellent. 'You'll write a book some day,' he said. Kemmy spent two years at the Christian Brothers school in Sexton Street and one year in the Technical School on O'Connell Avenue. Pat Reeves recalled: 'He was very good at school, always in the A stream in Sexton Street Christian Brothers.'

However, during Kemmy's teenage years, Michael Kemmy became severely ill and succumbed to tuberculosis.

'TB was raging through the city, it was very common,' said Pat Reeves. Tuberculosis, or TB for short, is a disease once common in Ireland, deadly infectious, often attacking the lungs, but also affects other parts of the body, being spread through the air. The battle to combat TB in Ireland was particularly led by Minister for Health at the time, Dr Noel Browne. A White Paper on health had resulted in the Health Act, 1947, introducing major reforms, which was forcefully implemented when Browne became Minister for Health soon after. The health reform coincided with the development of new drugs that helped to treat a previously untreatable group of medical conditions. Browne introduced mass free screening for tuberculosis sufferers and directed public resources to finance his anti-TB campaign, with improved medical and hospital services, dramatically reducing the incidence of tuberculosis in Ireland. But all too late for Michael Kemmy.

In an interview in later years with journalist Raymond Smith,[4] Jim Kemmy described how he watched his father die in a city hospital, 'a terrible death, wasting away to nothing, suffering horribly from bed sores towards the end, so it was unbearable for him to turn over'. In the hospital, Kemmy remembered an unsympathetic nun who did not help to ease the suffering of those final days. Some of these experiences may well have left him with a legacy of bitterness for future years. The death of his father certainly had an immediate effect on Jim Kemmy, the eldest of a family of five, three boys and two girls. He was 16 at the time and was forced to leave school to fend for his family. 'Certain events change you for life. I became a committed socialist. I could never change.'

Anna-Maria Hajba, the University of Limerick archivist who established the Kemmy Collection from his papers, told the author that this experience seems to have left an indelible mark on Jim Kemmy's character:

> Jim Kemmy was very committed to what he did, no half measures, everything or nothing, his trade union activities were on equal standing with his politics. His father died when he was very young, he had to take responsibility at a very young age. I can see that sense of responsibility extending to everything else, he became the defender of other people, early involvement in the trade unions, He never left his family down, sense of empowering people, it was very important for him to be in a position to help people.

These comments were echoed by others:[5] 'Jim Kemmy's politics were shaped by his life experiences. His experience of early poverty marked him all his life. When his father was sick, Jim was the only family member old enough to visit him'. Thus, while the Kemmy family was not necessarily materially impoverished, this early crisis would have placed the family under considerable strain and distress, leaving a memory that would have conditioned Kemmy's outlook throughout the rest of his life.

Following the death of his father, Jim Kemmy was indentured into the stonemason's trade, with an apprenticeship for seven years. Pat Reeves reported: 'I brought Jim to his first job, building new houses for Limerick City Council on Carey's Road.' Later, Kemmy went to work for private builders, looking for a wage increase shortly after his father's death, but claiming to Raymond Smith that he was dismissed for that request.

The 1950s was a decade of high unemployment and even the most skilled stonemasons found it difficult to secure work. Kemmy reported being frequently unemployed. The longest period was for six months, after which he took the emigrant ship to Britain in 1957, bolstered by his qualification as a stonemason. This experience of emigration influenced him to write a poem, although he never regarded it as a poem, but rather as a poetic statement, calling it 'Exiled Memory 57',[6] echoing the loneliness and confusion of the young Irish emigrants at the time:

Life-long dwindling to
That lone option;
The inescapable move
For survival and self-respect,
Forced out to a 'pagan' world
By hopeless unemployment.
Numbed, confused family parting.
Unreal train journey to Dublin,
Uninvited visit from young
Legion of Mary girl
Asking well-rehearsed questions
Last bitter look from Dun Laoghaire
Sickening loneliness and disillusionment
Of boat crossing
Long, restless haul from Holyhead.
Bleak, 6.45 am arrival at Euston,
Tired, dirty, nervous,
First, startling sight of black workers,
Awkwardness on underground escalator.
Smells and noises of station.

Emotional shock at sexy posters.
Blurred, strange names flashing past
Fogged windows of subway train.
Fighting down a galloping panic
And desire to catch the next train home.
Solitary search for a room and job
In bewildering places among self-absorbed people.
Relentless feelings of inadequacy
Crowding and clouding the mind.
Yearning for the stability of the familiar.
Cornered by fear of the unknown.
Straining for a homely voice
Or a helping hand.
Choked with homesickness.
Hoping for the best.
Fearing the worst.
Holding on . . .

Several themes come through clearly in this piece: the isolation of young people in a strange city combined with the shock of a foreign culture, together with the contradictory emotions of hope, fear, inadequacy and homesickness. Significantly, religious issues appear too, reference to the 'pagan' world and the Legion of Mary, although Kemmy's emerging atheism is clear in this poem – the religious references are very much outside himself, simply observations of external actors, and no suggestion is made of any internalised religious feelings on his own part.

In London, it was not unusual for the Irish to sleep five in a room. The first place Jim Kemmy stayed was run by a Mrs Cocking, a Welsh woman. The beds used by the Irish at night were not left idle during the day, being let out to long-distance coach and truck drivers coming from Wales to London, anxious to catch a few hours sleep. The beds, in effect, were being used for double shifts. 'I was in London at the time myself,' reported Margaret O'Donoghue, 'and people were actually sleeping on hammocks in those places, taking turns.'

Jim Kemmy was profoundly influenced by the London experience. Working on the building sites, he shared experiences with English workers, was introduced to the culture of the trade union movement, with many of his co-workers holding socialist and 'left-wing' views. Kemmy found his outlook broadening in English society, gaining a strong feeling for fellow-exiles down on their luck who could not cope with the forces of life away from their own land. Dan Miller told the author:

> For Jim, his real education was in Britain on the building sites. Jim once said 'building sites are tough places to grow up in, so if you can hold your own in that sort of situation, you know what you can do'. He spent a lot of his free time in libraries, this was his way of enjoying himself, not much money after sending his wages home, there was a huge influence of left-wing writers, although he would have read other right-wing writers as well.

According to Joe Kemmy:

> There was a massive change in Jim going to England. He was able to see through his own eyes that we needed to broaden our horizons, from the standpoint of London, he began to understand the class system in Limerick, became conscious of what he saw to be the inequalities and class divisions in his own city.

Pat Reeves confirmed the transformation that the London experience wrought on Kemmy:

> The Kemmys were a bright family, all of them bright sparks, but a quiet family, not radical at all. Growing up in Limerick, Jim had no interest in trade unions. He was called 'Seamus' in school and in the early years in Limer-

ick, but he came back from London as 'Jim'. Jim Kemmy really started reading in England, the English experience transformed him, he came back an atheist and a socialist. The impact of London was massive.

Joe Kemmy explained how his brother was struck by how people became class-conscious in London. People would vote Fianna Fáil in Ireland, yet would vote Labour in London. There was an awakening consciousness among the Irish in London and Jim Kemmy believed that nationalism had a major impact in diverting people from socialism. He saw west of Ireland people voting Labour in England, but returning to Ireland and voting for Fianna Fáil. The London atmosphere thus provided a rich environment for political awareness, although not necessarily sustained among the emigrants who returned.

In England, he began to read more and more. Reflecting in later years, Kemmy reported that the only book mentioned on the building sites was *Stone Mad* by the sculptor Seamus Murphy (1950), a study of stone cutting. Murphy was a successful sculptor whose book celebrating the work of the 'Stonies' has been described as a classic, serving as a tribute to the work of innumerable anonymous craftsmen in a tradition that had continued from medieval times, but whose craft had begun to die out in the 1940s. This had a strong influence on Kemmy, highlighting the importance of stone, and the human stories behind it. In the evenings, he would exchange books with his fellow lodgers. In this way was Kemmy also introduced to the works of John Steinbeck, the American author who was awarded the Pulitzer Prize in 1940 and the Nobel Prize for Literature in 1962. Kemmy found Steinbeck a 'different kind of writer, with working class sympathies, writing with realism about the itinerant farmworkers of California'.[7] The Steinbeck book that particularly influenced Kemmy was *The Grapes of*

Wrath, a novel published in 1939. Set during the Great Depression, the novel focuses on a poor family of sharecroppers, the Joads, driven from their Oklahoma home by drought, economic hardship and changes in the agriculture industry. In a nearly hopeless situation, they set out for California along with thousands of other 'Okies' in search of land, jobs and dignity. This experience of the 'Okies' sharply resonated with Kemmy's emerging socialist thinking, something he could easily relate to the Irish emigrant tradition.

A further book awakening his awareness at this time was *The Ragged Trousered Philanthropists* by Robert Tressell, first published in 1914, a controversial critique of capitalism in the workplace, and a seminal influence on the modern trade union movement in Britain. Tressell's cast of hypocritical Christians, exploitative capitalists and corrupt councillors provide a backdrop for his main target, the workers who think that a better life is 'not for the likes of them', hence the title of the book. Tressell paints the workers as 'philanthropists' who throw themselves into back-breaking work for poverty-level wages in order to generate profit for their masters. The hero of the book is a socialist who believes that the capitalist system is the real source of the poverty he sees all around him. In vain he tries to convince his fellow workers of his world view, but finds that their education has trained them to distrust their own thoughts and to rely on those of their 'betters'. This challenge of worker consciousness immediately impacted on Jim Kemmy, highlighting for him how, in the Irish case, the republican and clerical traditions had masked and clouded the real interests of the workers.

From an Irish perspective, James Connolly's *Labour in Irish History* (1910) was another building block in Kemmy's socialist consciousness. Connolly, a socialist, had been one of the executed leaders of the Irish rebellion of 1916, although he had distanced himself from the republican and nationalist volunteers, establishing instead the Irish Citizen Army, a group of armed volunteers whose aim was to defend workers and strikers. In his book, Connolly argued that Irish independence would bring little in the way of freedom and progress for the majority of the Irish people unless it included a fundamental challenge to the structure of society. Connolly claimed that the Irish capitalist class was always prepared to abandon and betray the struggle for liberation if its economic and social interests were threatened. In Jim Kemmy's mind, this argument by Connolly forcefully integrated the British and American worker traditions into the Irish situation, creating a clear perception for the future.

Speakers' Corner in Hyde Park provided a further stimulus to Kemmy's thinking. The open debates, fresh thinking and flux of ideas all excited him, standing in sharp contrast to the narrow and enclosed culture that he had left behind in Ireland. Kemmy's experiences in London introduced him to a strong tradition of trade union socialism, with concerns about the control of power and wealth in society, organisation of labour, ownership of economic institutions, meaning of democracy, equal opportunities, exploitation of workers and a host of related issues, all of which would immerse him for the rest of his life. This transformation in Kemmy's outlook may well have been echoed by the experiences of other Irish emigrants, reflecting a wider process. This was the ability of returning emigrants to bring new ideas and fresh thinking back to their home country, and was something that definitely enriched Ireland's development in the 1960s and 1970s, helping to 'internationalise' the Irish view of themselves in the world, whether in business, politics or social affairs – or trade union socialism in Kemmy's particular case.

Jim Kemmy returned to Limerick in 1960, carrying with him a range of impressions and new ideas, reflected in his luggage, a battered brown suitcase laden with books. His second poem, written at that time, 'Making a Comeback, 1960', reflected many of the contradictory sensations felt by the returned emigrant:

A jolt from sleep to consciousness
As the train slows at the
Yellow-washed Killonan station-house.
The glimpse of St John's spire
Through the thick, green foliage,
Noon arrival at Limerick station,
Filled with pain of departures,
Home to Garryowen, without glory.

Family greetings and accounts of London,
Surge of forgotten Limerick accents,
Change of pace and faces,
Unreal feeling, frozen in time,
Long restless Saturday afternoon,
Driving urge to go downtown,
Through the gateway of John's square,
To explore the incessant city.
O'Mahony's bookshop, first stop,
To buy 'The Collegians'
Poor, lonely Gerald Griffin –
You deserved better from life and death –
The sumptuous Savoy . . . memories of the
Sunday night picture and a box of Black Magic,
Café Capri, haunt of young romantics with
High hopes on a Coca Cola and a cake!

William Street encounter with Paddy Flynn,
Long time chairman of the Masons' Union,
Wounded response in Bryan Greene's bar,
'I will not crawl for a job . . .'

Take it easy now . . . stay at home..
Things have improved a lot here . . .
To sleep in your own bed
Is worth a lot in life'.

Mind filled with words and confusion,
'Take it easy . . . stay here . . .'
Home for tea and Radio Luxembourg,
Switch to Radio Eireann and
Back to a 1950s time warp,
'The Balladmakers Saturday Night',
And later, after 'Ceili House',
To sleep in my own bed.[8]

This second poem reflects well the changes in Kemmy's outlook – the influence of three years in London, the returning emigrant, the new thinking, the emerging social activist, the growing anger and indignation. There seems to be much disappointment, references to 'pain of departure' and 'without glory' suggest considerable frustration with the London experience. Talk about 'unreal feelings, frozen in time' almost suggest the shock of the returned emigrant, perhaps as confused with the homecoming as with his initial departure to England. The inner anger and antagonism of the young socialist is clear from 'I will not crawl for a job' but with others urging him to 'take it easy', the contradictory sensations of the home-comer are evident, trying to cope with the reality of his new situation. The London experience had opened up new vistas for Kemmy, seeing Ireland now in a different and much more critical light: 'back to a 1950s time warp'.

Perhaps disappointingly, Kemmy does not appear to have attempted any further poetry in later years. Certainly he seems to have had good talent in putting his feelings into words, with a strong insight and structured flow of ideas, but this was not a talent he tried to develop subsequently. Possibly the heavy demands of his political and trade union calling, and his interests in historical writing, absorbed him fully and diverted his attention from poetry.

Reflecting these early days of Kemmy and his return to Limerick, Brendan Halligan of the *Limerick Leader* told the author:

> The Jim Kemmy I first met in the mid-sixties was a big teddy bear of a man – warm, easy-going, comfortable to be with. We quickly became close friends. His London legacy soon surfaced. He was besotted by politics, not least British politics. He personified what London would now regard as Old Labour. There was no indication then of some of the causes with which he would become to be identified: the Two Nations theory, contraception, divorce, abortion . . .

A further legacy of Kemmy's London period was a dramatic change in his religious outlook. Although growing up a Catholic in Limerick, he developed a completely different view in Britain. With his many readings, he began to see religion as bogus: the evolutionary theories of Darwin, the sorry tales of religious persecution in the Spanish Inquisition, the politics of Rome – all conspired in Kemmy a view that religion was utter fiction. 'At the beginning he would have been a soft atheist, maybe accepting that just because you could not disprove the existence of God, did not necessarily mean God didn't exist, he was agnostic,' said Joe Kemmy. But Jim Kemmy's views developed to reject any supernatural existence and he grew to see the 'after life' as pure fantasy.

However Jim Kemmy never made any particular crusade about his non-belief. He never wrote about it, and his political focus was on the tangible implications, such as separation of Church and State. 'He worked well with many clerics who shared his social concerns, but he saw their religious message as pure nonsense,' said Joe Kemmy. How did his mother, an ardent churchgoer, react? According to Joe Kemmy:

> Mother didn't pay too much attention, when Jim was living with her he didn't push it, she had a good relationship with the clergy, and she didn't intrude on Jim's views. Once, she was asked by a local clergyman whether Jim was attending church 'you'd better ask him' she curtly retorted.

Other factors also influenced Kemmy throughout his life, perhaps the most durable being his relationship with his friend Patsy Harrold. Originally from Broad Street in Limerick, Patsy worked in the civil service, and was married to Fintan, with six children. She was always an enthusiastic reader, devouring the *Irish Times* and *Sunday Times*. Patsy was active in the local archaeological society, and committed to the anti-apartheid movement, once joining a march organised by Kemmy. Patsy told the author:

> 1974 was a very exciting local election – divorce, family planning, growing socialist movement. I met Jim first when he came to the house with election leaflets, he was very anti-conservation at the time, anti-taisce, liked to see building going on. So with my archaeological interests, there were lots for us to argue about.

On the death of his mother, Kemmy started coming for dinner to the Harrold household. Fintan died in 1976. Patsy reported that, following the death of her husband:

> Jim had a kind of a home here, but his real home was at the trade union offices, he was always out at meetings. Jim moved all his books here in Corbally, but going back sometimes to Garryowen, Jim was always lazy about his domestic arrangements.

Patsy worked actively with Jim Kemmy in many of his heritage and political initiatives, the two sharing a strong and enriching companionship over twenty years.

Patsy's son Seamus Harrold told the author:

> His mother died in 1974, so Jim was a lonely single man in Garryowen, he started coming more and more to our household. He was like a father to me, and he helped with money during the illness of my father, he was great backbone, he was so straight and direct, no nonsense, we all learnt real honesty from Jim. He spent more and more time with us, would stay a night or a week end, it became longer and longer. Of course he wasn't whiter than white, he could certainly be lazy if he wanted to. For example, Jim was best man at my wedding, but he broke my heart, he turned up late at the church, just getting there before the bride, without a flower in his lapel, he had to rob one from the priest's garden!

Endnotes

1. *Limerick Leader*, 9 March 1963.

2. 'Tribute to Jim Kemmy', compiled by Luke Verling (Earth Productions, Dublin, 1999).

3. *Old Limerick Journal*, 1998.

4. *Garret: The Enigma - Dr Garret Fitzgerald* by Raymond Smith (Aherlow Publishers, Dublin, 1985).

5. Luke Verling, 1999.

6. *Old Limerick Journal*, Winter 1989.

7. *Influences* by Jim Kemmy, undated note (Kemmy Collection, University of Limerick).

8. *Old Limerick Journal*, 1989.

2

Jim Kemmy Enters Politics

Labour Party in the 1960s

Kemmy returned to Limerick in 1960 at the dawn of the new economic and industrial boom. Following some work in Cement Ltd in Limerick, he was employed in building one of the first factories at Shannon Industrial Estate (later moving in 1965 to employment as a stonemason by Limerick City Council, where he worked until 1981, leaving then to concentrate on his political and trade union commitments). Jim Kemmy's return to Limerick at that time was marked by his entry to the Labour Party, spurred by the socialist ideas assimilated in the London building sites. Kemmy rose rapidly in the ranks of the Labour Party, soon becoming a member of the National Administrative Council and local director of elections in Limerick. Patsy Harrold told the author, 'Jim in those days was into everything, a real passionate radical, he could never stop going, bursting with energy.'

This energy was soon evident. In 1969/70, he set up a socialist study group in Limerick, debating political issues and inviting external speakers, many with prominent national profiles at the time, such as Bernadette Devlin (political activist from Northern Ireland), Conor Cruise O'Brien (academic, Labour

Party, later minister) and Noel Browne. Kemmy's brand of socialism was reported not to extend to the Irish Communist Organisation, and he was not a member of that organisation, disagreeing with their fundamental approach, although he did share some common views with them, particularly on the need for Church–State separation and recognition of Northern Ireland, according to Luke Verling.[1] Although Joe Kemmy told the author that his brother had in fact a lot in common with the Irish Communist Organisation, and admired many of their policies, 'Jim did not join the ICO, it was not politically active enough'.

The Labour Party in the early 1960s was a movement with distinct features, according to a history by Michael Gallagher,[2] operating in a political and social environment not conducive to the emergence of a strong socialist party. The loyalties created by Fianna Fáil and Fine Gael in the early years of the state, following the civil war, transcended class divisions, and were transmitted to succeeding generations. The most basic cleavage between the two main parties sprung from the split in the nationalist party early in the century. The 1916 rebellion, war of independence up to 1921 and the civil war of 1922-23 left a political legacy where issues of nationalism and republicanism dominated the political agenda. Thus the absence of a tradition of serious political debate on socio-economic questions meant that the two larger parties denied that terms like 'left' or 'right' had any meaning in the context of the society in which they operated. This gave Labour the problem of fighting an uphill battle against general indifference. Furthermore, the social structure of the Irish Republic could not be expected to generate a strong socialist party. The objectively defined 'working class' was not large by the standards of modern industrial societies.

By 1969, the Labour Party as a whole contained three distinct groups: the traditional rural right, the pro-coalition left and the anti-coalition left. The problems of transition were beginning to manifest themselves. Of 17 Labour TDs in 1970, nine represented Dublin constituencies and eight were from rural constituencies; eight had university degrees and nine did not; nine had entered the Parliamentary Labour Party since 1965 and eight had become members earlier. This was the Labour Party which Kemmy joined in the early 1960s. Dan Miller explained to the author: 'Jim's entry to the Labour Party coincided with the addition of several very high-profile new members from the intelligentsia: Conor Cruise O'Brien, Justin Keating, David Thornley. Jim would have been attracted by this new blood at the time.'

Niall Greene of the Labour Party told the author: 'The 1968 annual conference was definitely anti-coalition, some people even going so far as to argue that anybody advocating coalition should be "booted out" of the party. There was no room for any pro-coalitionist in the Labour Party until after 1970.' However, Niall Greene reported that he did not recall Kemmy ever being against coalition in principle: 'Jim Kemmy was much too progressive a political activist for that.'

The tensions between the traditionalists and newcomers inherent in the Labour Party at this time were brought out very clearly by the argument over Stephen Coughlan in 1970. Dick Spring explained to the author:

> The relationship between Jim Kemmy and the Labour Party was very difficult in the early days. There were a number of factions in Limerick: Coughlan, the extreme left and Kemmy's group. The Labour Party in rural Ireland was very conservative in social affairs, this would have been a source of conflict, making it very difficult for everyone.

Coughlan, the Labour TD in Limerick, had incurred the animosity of many Labour members by a number of actions.

He had criticised anti-apartheid campaigners and, as mayor, had hosted an official reception for a visiting South African rugby team, in the face of active protest from other members of the Labour Party, including Kemmy. At the time, the South African policy of 'apartheid' (enforced racial segregation) was attracting much international opposition. A further contro- versy ocurred when Coughlan warned a left-wing group in Limerick (the 'Maoists' – an extreme socialist splinter group, taking their aims from Mao Tse Tung, then chairman of the Chinese Communist Party) that they should leave the city before they were 'crushed without mercy'. When a shot was later fired at a bookshop operated by the Maoists, Cough- lan issued a statement condemning not the violence but the bookshop, which he termed a 'deliberate provocation' to the people of Limerick, since the Maoists were 'completely op- posed to our Christian traditions'. Labour's National Admin- istrative Council (of which Kemmy was by then a member), responded to calls from Dublin members for the expulsion of Coughlan and issued its own statement. But this also seemed more concerned about the existence of the bookshop than the violence used against it, generating further criticism from Dublin members.

The tension between Kemmy and Coughlan was palpable and continuous. Niall Greene told the author that during the 1968 by-election following the death of Donagh O'Malley (lo- cal Fianna Fáil Minister for Education), Kemmy:

> . . . fired Coughlan off the campaign, Jim Kemmy was di- rector of elections for Labour in East Limerick and told Coughlan to 'go home'. Coughlan was not pulling his weight, at least in Kemmy's eyes, maybe because Cough- lan felt threatened by the new Labour candidate, Mick Lipper.

The dispute finally erupted in April 1970 when Coughlan made a speech to the Credit Union League of Ireland. After praising the role of credit unions because they made reliance on moneylenders unnecessary, he gave his retrospective endorsement to a campaign conducted against Limerick Jews in 1904, and urged people to join a credit union instead of being exploited by 'extortionist warble-fly bloodsuckers'. There was a flood of calls from Dublin branches for his expulsion. Brendan Corish, then leader of the Labour Party, repudiated his remarks at once, saying that anti-semitism was repugnant to the Irish people and to the Labour Party. However, the Parliamentary Labour Party voted overwhelming against withdrawing the whip from him, although Coughlan, at its instigation, did issue an apology in which he stated 'I sincerely regret the words I used'. This apology was accepted by the Chief Rabbi of Ireland, although he added that he was distressed by the shocking outburst of anti-Jewish remarks. The Labour Administrative Council was then presented with a motion to expel Coughlan, but this was defeated by a narrow margin. In response to this, four left-wing members, including Jim Kemmy, resigned from the Administrative Council and left the meeting, while those remaining adopted a statement which endorsed Corish's rejection of the 'recent anti-semitic remarks of Alderman Stephen Coughlan, TD', implying that only the Chief Rabbi's acceptance of his apology had forestalled stronger measures, and warning that any party members repeating such views would incur 'immediate expulsion'.

Certainly there was widespread realisation that party unity was in danger. Indeed, at one point in the initial stages of the affair Coughlan threatened that if he were expelled he would form a new version of the Labour Party, which could have attracted some of Labour's more conservative supporters. While a minority would have been glad to see him and those of like mind leave the party, a majority, while not necessarily taking Coughlan's threat seriously, wanted to prevent rather than force a split, according to Michael Gallagher.

Niall Greene told the author:

> There was a very high regard for Jim within the Labour National Administrative Council, especially held by Brendan Corish, the then leader. In April 1970 the Parliamentary Party and the Administrative Council disciplined Coughlan, and disowned him for his anti-semitic remarks, but did not expel him from the party.

With Jim Kemmy, Matt Merrigan and Brendan Scott, Niall Greene (who was then the Party treasurer) resigned from the Administrative Council, 'although maybe in hindsight that was a bit over the top,' said Greene.

Later that year, Niall Greene successfully stood against Kemmy in an election for the post of vice-chairman of the Labour Party. Greene was very much supported by the 'establishment' of the Labour Party. He said: 'Since the 1960s the Labour Party was very much in flux with a take-over of the party by a new, younger and more radical generation, including Jim Kemmy.'

In Limerick, clashes between Coughlan and Kemmy were frequent, reflecting the different political philosophies of the two men. Coughlan was conservative, opposed to legalisation for divorce or contraception, both of which Kemmy supported. Tension persisted between the two. In spite of that, Kemmy remained active during the 1960s, being local organising secretary of the party in Limerick, and maintaining his connections with the National Administrative Council. In these early years, Jim Kemmy did not appear to harbour electoral ambitions as such; instead, he focused on local politics and national policies. He was also very involved in making representations on behalf of local residents to assist them in their domestic and personal difficulties. Kemmy continued with his educational development, completing in 1967 a two-year extramural diploma in Social Science from University College Cork in the School of Commerce on Mulgrave Street. This educational experience certainly seems to have provided him with substantial resources, as his writing and speeches after-wards displayed improved structure and coherence, while he maintained his left-wing views.

Eventually, the ongoing controversies with Coughlan proved too much, and Kemmy resigned from the Labour Party in 1972, bringing 40 members with him. Kemmy's statement at the time was that the Labour Party was not a socialist party, and that it would never bring about socialism in Ireland. Frank Prender-gast, senior member of the Labour Party in Limerick, said that he was saddened to see Jim Kemmy leave the party. However, while Prendergast knew what Kemmy's principles had cost him, he believed that Kemmy was mistaken in resigning, as 'no person ever improves an organisation by leaving it'.[3]

Niall Greene told the author:

> Jim gradually became distanced from the Labour Party. He was highly regarded at national level, his problem was on the ground in Limerick and dealing with what he saw to be the very conservative and regressive forces within the Limerick Labour group. Jim set up a local so-cialist group against this local resistance, so it was a way of clearing the local blockage. Jim was always regarded by the national people as somebody difficult to deal with, but was hugely respected.

According to Joe Kemmy, there were much wider issues leading to Jim Kemmy's disillusionment with the Labour Par-ty than Coughlan alone. For example, Kemmy believed firmly that the problem of Northern Ireland demanded a 'two na-tions' settlement on the island of Ireland: an Ulster nation and a southern Irish nation. According to Kemmy, Ulster Unionists should be given the right to opt out of a united Ireland, but Labour continued to maintain a strong anti-partition and republican theme in its policies. Also, many in the Labour Party were hostile to EU membership, a development that Kemmy ardently supported. Kemmy's strong view was that the EU provided a vital vehicle for worker solidarity and should be embraced as a matter of urgency. Overall, Jim Kemmy believed the Labour Party was stagnant: many developments were happening around it, such as the Dublin Housing Action Committee (an active protest group against poor housing conditions in Dublin), but Labour members were isolating themselves from these important movements, Jim Kemmy believed. All this, plus the conflict with Coughlan, rendered it impossible for Kemmy to stay in the party.

Dan Miller echoed this wider issue to the author:

> Jim Kemmy left Labour because of coalition with Fine Gael. Kemmy believed that the Left should stay together, rather than go into coalition with Fine Gael. At the time, we thought it was the right thing to do, but with hindsight Jim might have had regrets about the split with Labour, maybe we could have changed Labour better from the inside.

Brendan Halligan of the *Limerick Leader* told the author:

> Jim regarded Steve Coughlan as a 'Vincent de Paul socialist' – if indeed he regarded him as a socialist at all – addressing the results of socioeconomic injustice rather than the causes. By contrast, Jim was a classic socialist. In the late Sixties or very early Seventies he travelled to Moscow. He wasn't a fellow-traveller, however. Nor did he return as a convert to communism. He never favoured statism or state capitalism. He leaned more towards syndicalism,[4] which explains his later espousal of industrial

democracy. In his early thirties he seemed destined to be a mainstream Labour politician, not a maverick. But there was a problem. Intelligent, articulate and committed, he was seen as a threat to Steve Coughlan. And Steve wasn't going anywhere soon.

The Coughlan controversy, and Kemmy's growing disillusionment with the Labour Party, began at this stage to galvanise his political ideas, reflecting a growing political awareness.

Independent Candidate

Following his departure from the Labour Party, Kemmy established with others the Limerick Socialist Organisation. In 1974, he stood as an independent candidate in the local elections and was elected to Limerick City Council on first count with 1,275 votes. This was reported to be the highest ever recorded by a candidate contesting the local government elections for the first time, reflecting the growing base of support in the Limerick area for Kemmy. A key supporter in all this was his brother, Joe. According to Dan Miller:

> Joe, his brother, was a great 'leveller' for Jim, Joe was the organiser, the listener. Jim learnt a lot from Joe, there was massive depth of trust between them, Jim Kemmy would have trusted Joe implicitly.

Manus O'Riordan confirmed this:

> His brother Joe was the backbone of Jim Kemmy. Jim would be out on the campaign, totally sucked into personal concerns, political issues and controversies, Joe was the organisation behind his brother, Jim would stay all night on a doorstep talking politics, but Joe would move him on to the next appointment, Joe was the manager all the time.

Seamus Harrold told the author:

> Joe Kemmy was calling all the shots, he was very astute.
> Joe was the master tactician, Jim would do the slogging
> on the ground. Joe Kemmy knew how to get the 'machine'
> out, we were very well briefed, never ask for a vote di-
> rectly, just say 'think of Jim', you might get the number
> two vote, never get into an argument, if there was an issue
> take the name and address.

Dan Miller told the author about the group of people who
collected around Kemmy:

> There was great vibrancy in those times, imagine a bunch
> of us in a pub, great discourse and discussion, all of us
> young apprentices really influenced by Jim and his imagi-
> nation and visions, even the intonations in their speech,
> the young people borrowed from Jim. Jim was very clever
> in his dealings with people. He would use psychology, if
> he disagreed with you, he would ignore your point, but if
> you said something he supported, he would immediately
> back you loudly: 'that's right, that's right'. He was very ef-
> fective in getting people to understand their situation.

Steve Coughlan lost his seat in 1977 to the new Labour candidate, Mick Lipper. Looking back on this period in a later decade, Kemmy reported that Coughlan was a robust, flamboy-
ant and colourful character. 'He was sometimes over the top
and sometimes his own worst enemy, but that was part and
parcel of his make-up. I had my differences with him when I
joined the party. I suppose I was young and too impatient. Socially, I would describe him as conservative.' reflected Kemmy,
following the death of Steve Coughlan in 1994.[5]

In that 1977 election, Kemmy targetted the Labour seat in
the Limerick East constituency. Although failing to win a seat,
Kemmy's support was beginning to build up, with his local

work, and his trade union connections, starting to bear fruit, as evidenced by this quote from a local newsletter:

> As the only regular newspaper appearing in this area, the *Southill Star* has a major responsibility in deciding to give its support to only one candidate . . . the *Star* has no hesitation unreservedly giving its support to Jim Kemmy. No other candidate has a record of work for the people to compare with Kemmy's.[6]

Kemmy's election literature at the time is significant, setting out his political philosophy on several issues: Northern Ireland, family planning, separation of Church and State and democratic control of schools.

At that time, articles 2 and 3 of the Irish Constitution claimed that the 'national territory consisted of the whole island of Ireland', and that any laws passed in the Republic would be without prejudice to the right of the Dáil to exercise jurisdiction over the whole island. This was effectively a political claim to Northern Ireland. Although, in reality, much of this anti-partitionism was 'rhetoric', according to historians, and opinion in the Republic was covertly realistic, the predominant note of the Republic of Ireland at the time was 'to look after its own'.[7] However, Kemmy believed that any solution to the Northern Ireland problem was to be found in recognition of the right of the Northern Ireland Protestant majority to opt for a state of their own choosing, with safeguards for the rights of Catholics. Kemmy was a member of the small but vociferous 'Socialists against Nationalism' group, vehement critics of the traditional nationalist approach, which, they argued, was a barrier to the development of working class unity in the north. They advocated a recognition by the southern state that the northern majority had a right to self-determination. This was the 'two nations theory' – a radical statement for its time. Ultimately, in later years, the two offending constitutional articles were modified by referendum in 1998 to include the principle of consent: 'A united Ireland shall be brought about only by peaceful means with the consent of a majority of the people, democratically expressed, in both jurisdictions in the island.' Although falling short of the 'two nations' idea, this principle of consent certainly came very close to the views advocated by Jim Kemmy, and his lobbying over the years must thus have been one of the instrumental factors in the creation of an awareness about the Northern Ireland realities. He certainly was an important influence within the Labour movement in this direction, and one of the significant building blocks in the new policy.

Manus O'Riordan, then a member of BICO (British and Irish Communist Party), told the author how he became politically involved with Kemmy from 1971 onwards. Jim Kemmy had a practice of organising in Limerick debates among the socialist groups on key issues and controversies within the socialist movement, and hosted several meeting and workshops. BICO participated, and valued very much Kemmy's open approach in stimulating debate and discussion on the important issues of the day, according to Manus O'Riordan.

BICO at that time had been promoting this 'two nations theory', Kemmy being very attracted by this principle, with the result in 1972 of the formation of the Workers Alliance for Democratic Settlement of the Northern Ireland Conflict. According to Manus O'Riordan: 'That sounds a mouthful, but the essential idea was very important: the only way to promote peace was through the principle of recognition of the right of the northern unionists to opt out, with the principle of consent.'

Dan Miller explained to the author:

> We interacted with People's Democracy in Northern Ireland (a secular left-wing group in the 1970s, outside the nationalist mainstream), we had discourses on the

Malone Road in Belfast, a whole host of people clus-
tered around Jim Kemmy, a lot of wonderful debates not
just about Northern Ireland, but about the meaning of
politics.

This stance against nationalism was a consistent feature of
Kemmy's life. At one point, the Limerick Trades Council requested the Irish Congress of Trade Unions to send a delegation of trade unionists to Northern Ireland to protest against
treatment of republican prisoners. But Jim Kemmy proposed
an amendment to include condemnation of the Provisional
IRA 'who are trying to impose a solution on Northern Ireland'.[8] On another occasion, at the time of the Pope's visit to
Ireland, Kemmy called on the hierarchy to impress upon the
Pope the urgency of calling on the Provisional IRA to end its
campaign of violence in the North when he visits the country.
'The Provisional IRA are a Catholic army and I am convinced
that an appeal by the Pope will have a salutary effect.'[9]

This reference to the Pope suggested another of Kemmy's
themes: his persistent call for the separation of Church and
State, coming from his desire for a more secular and non-de-
nominational society. The Catholic Church had made substantial progress since Vatican II, particularly in promoting
enlightened social policies and assistance to the Third World,
working towards a 'conscience of society' model. However,
traditional teaching was still dominant, with strong features
of Catholic 'majoritarianism' still persisting.[10] In Kemmy's
view, the Catholic Church enjoyed an excessively powerful
and domineering position in Irish society, which he sought
to counterbalance through a socialist model of Church–State
separation. In the 1970s, Kemmy's was one of the few strident
voices calling so loudly for such a shift.

Kemmy's call for family planning reflected a strengthening
mood for change. Under the Criminal Law Amendment Act

of 1935, it was illegal to import or sell contraceptives, the 'pill' being only available on prescription. However, the Family Planning Association had developed a network of clinics and reported substantial demand. Kemmy was one of a growing group that called for further liberalisation at this time, and he was active in helping to establish one of Ireland's first Family Planning Clinics at Cornmarket Row in Limerick in 1974. This was initially operated on a voluntary basis advising on contraceptive methods not requiring a doctor's prescription. Trade unionist Mike McNamara told the author: 'Returning from trade union meetings in Dublin, Kemmy would often bring with him on the train a large consignment of contraceptive supplies for the Limerick clinic.'

The clinic was later extended to provide a full medical service to include a doctor's advice on contraception, although, significantly, no doctors were available in Limerick and the clinic had to be staffed, until 1977, by a visiting physician from Dublin. The clinics provided an opportunity for family planning not otherwise available to people at that time, attracting 50 enquiries per week by 1976. Subsequently, in 1978, the Dáil voted through a modest reform, making contraceptives available, but restricted them to 'bona fide family planning purposes'. Under this legislation, by 1979, two doctors were available on scheduled times for medical clinics, with non-medical advice available at all times. In 1985, and in later years, the Government further liberalised the legislation on contraception.

Kemmy's perspective on the family planning controversy is illustrated by a later speech on the theme 'a new morality needed':

> One of the most disgusting sights during the present contraception debate has been that of deputies claiming that this matter is one of 'morality' and therefore needs

to be looked at in a different way from the other matters that come up in the Dáil. This shows a perverted definition of morality. Do people see no moral dimension in the perpetuation of an unjust and inequitable tax system? . . . There is no exalted morality involved in middle-aged politicians or bishops interfering in the private lives of our young people . . . it is time we developed a morality which is humane and civilised, based on respect and tolerance and not the craw-thumping intolerance of those who despise our young people.[11]

Separation of Church and State was also reflected in Kemmy's urging for democratic control of schools, and the need for what he saw to be public and community-based control of education, without Church influence. At the time, the Church's influence over education was relatively dominant: bishops were patrons of primary schools, parish priests had substantial influence over teacher appointments and religious orders exercised considerable management control over second-level education. This was a feature of the Irish education system that Kemmy continuously opposed. In later years, reflecting social and political change, the Church's impact was substantially diluted, such that, by 1998, the education legislation was recognising the duty of local boards of management to manage schools in the 'public interest'.

In 1977, Kemmy's views on Northern Ireland, family planning, separation of Church and State and democratic control of schools were very much minority positions, but since then have been substantially mainstreamed into public policy. Jim Kemmy therefore acted as a forerunner and precursor of many later reforms, helping to spearhead important pressures for change, particularly galvanising support for these changes within the labour movement. Furthermore, this intervention by an independent local public representative into national issues was unusual. Independent representatives in Ireland traditionally tended to focus on exclusively local issues, so Kemmy's interests in these wider affairs was a significant departure from prevailing practice.

According to Dan Miller, one of Kemmy's political supporters:

> Jim was passionate about engaging in controversies with others, especially if he did not share their views. Jim had a simple view: these people have a level of learning, if you can hold your own in an argument with them, you know you have a basis for your own views, we had loads of interplay with this approach. At one stage, Jim was about to join an industry association or grouping of some sort, but was warned off it by a colleague with the observation that there might be extreme religious groups involved, such as the Knights of Columbanus, to which he replied, 'nothing to be afraid of!' He thrived on controversy.

In the 1977 general election, Manus O'Riordan explained that many of the BICO members came to Limerick to campaign for Kemmy:

> Jim Kemmy had a real 'machine' going for him, with a brass band following him in the street led by somebody no less than Seán Bourke.[12] Seán sounded incongruous with his posh English accent calling on people 'to vote for Jim Kemmy and put Limerick on the map'. . . . BICO was not a hindrance to Jim Kemmy in that election, it may even have helped him, certainly his role in family planning was critical in garnering support.

Seamus Harrold told the author:

> In the 1977 elections, we were totally naïve, we thought people would vote for us once they said so, but that's not how the system works, we learnt eventually. Jim would be canvassing all night if he was allowed, doggedly going

after every vote. But it was Lipper against Coughlan competing for the Labour vote, Lipper winning, and Jim was squeezed out by the two of them.

Although failing in 1977, Jim Kemmy finally saw success in June 1981 with his election to the Dáil, defeating Mick Lipper, then the sitting Labour TD. Labour had mounted two candidates, Mick Lipper and Frank Prendergast. Kemmy received more first preferences than the either of the two Labour candidates, reflecting the growth of his support in the city, although the combined first preferences of the two Labour candidates exceeded Kemmy's. However, this advantage did not bring them any benefit as Kemmy attracted second preferences from many candidates, including his Labour opponents, ensuring his victory.[13] Niall Greene told the author:

> With the loss of the seat to Jim in 1981, many in the Labour Party thought it was terrible blow, but the reality was that there has only ever been only one seat available to the left in Limerick (apart from one term when there were two in the 1930s and for the 1957/61 term), and that seat could have been taken by Fianna Fáil or Fine Gael, so you could say that Jim was 'minding the seat' for Labour.

This election saw the installation of the coalition government of Labour and Fine Gael, led by Garret Fitzgerald. As a TD, Kemmy voted in support of the coalition, including an emergency budget introduced by the Minister for Finance, John Bruton, in July 1981.

For the following six months, Kemmy was active in the Dáil, making several contributions to different debates. In his first speech,[14] he castigated the main political parties for failing to develop a simple consensus around the appointment of the Ceann Comhairle (chairman) of the Dáil:

That is a cruel approach. My instincts would be on the side of fair play and democracy. In the last two Governments there has been a winner-take-all approach in regard to the appointment of Ceann Comhairle and Leas-Cheann Comhairle. I deplore this attitude. Unless we have some kind of civilised attitude in our approach to these appointments, which are non-contentious offices, we cannot point a finger at the North and talk about power sharing. We are very good at that and saying they should do this, that and the other. Our example is not very good. Perhaps we can learn something from what I have said.

He called for 'civilised and comprehensive divorce laws' to alleviate the distress and hardship caused by the then annulment system, which was divorce under a different name and caused what he saw to be tremendous problems, favouring the wealthy rather than the poor. At that time, the Irish Constitution of 1937 prohibited divorce by stipulating 'no law shall be enacted providing for the grant of dissolution of marriage' (in the following years, a referendum for divorce in 1986 was defeated, although the divorce measure was later approved in a subsequent 1995 referendum).

In a separate debate, Kemmy argued that calls for British withdrawal from Northern Ireland were harmful to relations between this country and Britain. Indeed, he claimed that these repeated calls for British withdrawal from Northern Ireland could be offensive to the one million British subjects in the North of Ireland to whom the sign 'Brits Out' was repugnant because 'they are British and Northern Irish just as the Welsh are Welsh and British and the Scottish are Scottish and British at the same time'.[15]

Speaking in a 1981 transport debate, Kemmy called for improved management and industrial relations at CIE, the national transport company. But the stonemason came out too:

I have a fondness, when travelling up and down to Dublin by rail, for looking at those Victorian railway stations built by the British. They are stations of great beauty and character. They are of beautiful design and stonework. We have not refurbished them too well. Our stone bridges, perhaps built under a different regime, are also very important. They give character to cities and towns and it is important to preserve them. I hope the Minister will look at that area.

In caustic tone, later in the year, he threw sharp invective at some other TDs:

I am not very impressed with the level of this debate. It reminds me of what I have read about undergraduate debating. I had not the opportunity of taking part in such debating as an undergraduate but I have read a good deal about the kind of debating which goes on and the kind of schoolboy arguments which go on at those debates . . . they are all sound and fury signifying nothing . . . employment, peace in the land, taxation equity, matters relating to women and family legislation in general are far more important than what we are discussing now.[16]

Kemmy was also active outside the Dáil at this stage. Speaking at a public meeting in 1981,[17] Kemmy argued that the absence of divorce had not prevented marriage breakdown. There had been an increase in marriage breakdown in Ireland but no divorce. Marriage breakdown was caused by a loosening of the bonds that make people put up with terrible situations. These bonds had been loosened by industrialisation, more wealth, changing religious values, increasing emancipation of women and other factors. To use a very gloomy parallel, said Kemmy, divorce was to marriage as funeral was to death. Divorce was the burial of a dead marriage, not the cause of the death.

In January 1982, the Fitzgerald government made prepa-
rations for the annual budget. Economic circumstances were
very difficult: unemployment was rising, economic growth
was poor and severe financial deficits limited the government's scope for action. The outlook was for a stringent set
of measures aiming to control the exchequer finances. The
balance of power in the Dáil between Fianna Fáil and the ruling Fine Gael/Labour coalition was held by a small number of
independent TDs, including Jim Kemmy.

Kemmy issued a statement[18] on his conditions for supporting the government's budget: 'In coming to a decision to back
Garret Fitzgerald in the vote for taoiseach, I bore in mind that
the electorate had swung heavily against a government with a
bad record.' However, Jim Kemmy also said that his mandate
was not one of uncritical support for the coalition parties. This
new government at best deserved a breathing space until the
budget before passing a more definite judgement on its inten-
tions. A 'yes' vote from Kemmy to the budget's social welfare
and taxation proposals would depend on several factors: increase in real value of social welfare payments; continuation
of food subsidies; maintenance of the top rate of income tax
on large incomes; a substantial increase in taxation of banks;
further capital taxation; in general, no shift from direct to indirect taxation. This reflected substantial negative feelings towards the budget. According to Seamus Harrold: 'Prior to the
1982 budget, we had a meeting in the Mechanics' Institute in
Limerick on the Sunday, with 20-30 supporters. We all said to
Jim he could not support the budget.'

Stephen O'Byrnes, in his history[19] of the Fine Gael party at
the time, described the ensuing events in some colour:

> Fitzgerald had meetings with Jim Kemmy and Noel
> Browne. They were alarmed at reports that the food sub-
> sidies were to go, and they told the taoiseach that they

would be unable to vote for such a measure. Fitzgerald listened, but gave no indication of his plans. He was quite obsessed about secrecy on the matter. That weekend, in a *Sunday Independent* interview, Kemmy publicly signalled that he would not vote for the budget the following Wednesday if the food subsidies were removed, or if there were further VAT increases. However, Fitzgerald was not too concerned. He calculated that Kemmy would not desert because the subsidies were only being modified, and welfare rise would offset the VAT rises for the less well-off.

The independent labour TD from Limerick was deeply upset. He had rung some of his close associates in Limerick, and they agreed with him that he could not support the budget. There was too little capital taxation; the food subsidies had major cuts; there was a new footwear and clothing tax. Kemmy had explained from the outset that he would not support the budget. Fitzgerald suggested something might be done on footwear and clothing. He gave Kemmy some pages he had drawn up showing the impact of the budget measures on people living on different incomes, showing how the less well off would benefit. Kemmy left with those and returned to his room. But he had not said he would be changing his mind.

The division bells rang for the first vote. Soon the chamber was filling up. Kemmy entered and went up to Fitzgerald. He returned the document to him and repeated he could not support the government. The division bells had now ceased and the chamber doors were locked. The deputies began to troop up the steps to the division lobbies, Government supporters wheeling left at the top, opposition turning right.

In the flurry and flux of so many people moving about and leaving their seats, nobody really noticed Fitzgerald as he headed across to Kemmy in the no-man's-land between the government and opposition benches. Now, he was actually kneeling on the bench in front of the Limerick man, talking earnestly and low to him. It was the posture of a supplicant.

Suddenly the packed press gallery noticed it. Word was already out that Kemmy might not back the government. Fitzgerald was pleading with him. He was shaking and distraught. But Kemmy had his mind made up. 'The die is cast,' he said. It was too late for further argument. Fianna Fáil deputies had also noticed the extraordinary scene. They began jeering and catcalling Fitzgerald. He drew up hurriedly from his kneeling posture, backing away like a child caught with his hand in the cookie jar. It was an ignominious, embarrassing exposure of the government's lack of political nous and professionalism.

For an eternity it seemed deputies were filing from their seats. Now they were down to a trickle. Only Kemmy, Sean Loftus and Joe Sherlock remained. Kemmy was the first to move. Slowly he reached the top. All eyes were on him. They had all seen Fitzgerald plead with him. Everyone realised the importance of what was happening. For the first time since he came into Leinster House seven months earlier, Kemmy turned right. There was as a gasp of excitement from the press gallery. Kemmy was followed by Sherlock and Loftus, bringing down the government by 82 votes to 81.

Was it avoidable? That was the immediate question. Kemmy was bitter. He felt he had been taken for granted. The man who had backed the government in all crucial divisions had clearly outlined his breaking point over the previous days and weeks. The government pleaded budget secrecy. But Fitzgerald and other ministers never believed that Kemmy would vote to put Haughey back in office. To that extent they had certainly taken him for granted.

There should have been a more formal structure for dealing with the independent deputies, who were crucial to the government's survival. Indeed, such a proposal had been put to a Fine Gael parliamentary party meeting previously, but the arrangement was never formalised.

This view that more could have been done to enlist Kemmy's support was reflected by Michael Gallagher, in his history of the Labour Party. Gallagher reported that, following the February 1982 election, the Labour Party held meetings in early March which produced a list of priorities, including modifying the harshest features of the budget. This belated stiffening of Labour's position was criticised by Jim Kemmy, who argued that what the party was now advocating was virtually the same as what he had called for before the budget. If the Labour ministers had stood up for themselves then, they could have ensured that the budget was acceptable to him and there would have been no election. There was, indeed, a widespread feeling that the budget defeat could have been avoided had the government been more adroit politically and more sensitive to the feelings of independent TDs.

Niall Greene told the author:

The fall of the government in 1982 was an extraordinary piece of ineptitude. People must have been asleep to think that the public would accept VAT on children's shoes, particularly as the government were reliant on independent TDs. They should have checked with the independents beforehand, the government was too rigid in their thinking.

Said Manus O'Riordan:

Jim Kemmy had stuck his neck out in supporting the unpopular 1981 budget. Noel Browne put a lot of pressure on Jim to support the government, but Jim had backed the government in 1981, and a line had to be drawn in the sand by the '82 budget.

However, there were alternative views to all this. Writing in the years after the event, Garret Fitzgerald[20] said he believed at the time that the independent deputies would be likely to support what would be the most radical and socially progressive – as well as the toughest – budget in the history of the State. It was designed to reduce the huge budget deficit left by Fianna Fáil, a process which had been started in the emergency budget introduced in July 1981, three weeks after the change of government. But it was also a budget of social reform. 'Prior to the budget I met them to hear their views – without, of course, being able to tell them of our plans.'

Kemmy had stated that he would support the budget only in the event of 'the continuation of food subsidies'. And, in relation to VAT, 'as a general principle', he would oppose 'any major shift from direct to indirect taxation: in particular there should be no increase in the lower rate of VAT.' The trouble, from Fitzgerald's perspective, was that if the government did not touch either food subsidies or VAT, they would be substantially short of the sums needed for their ambitious social reform and redistribution policies. According to Garret Fitzgerald:

> After the budget speech I met Jim Kemmy and Noel Browne, as well as a third non-socialist independent, Sean Loftus, to hear their reactions. Noel Browne clearly understood the social thrust of the budget and said he would support it, and Mr Loftus said little or nothing, giving no indication of dissatisfaction. Jim Kemmy, however, was clearly unhappy. Unlike Noel Browne, he did not seem to appreciate the extent to which this was a redistributive budget. In particular, he rejected any reduction whatever in food subsidies.

Fitzgerald also reported that the issue of VAT on clothing and footwear was not raised by Kemmy, either in that discussion or in the immediate post-budget statement he made to the media after its defeat. Indeed, before the vote on the budget, the issue of VAT on clothing and children's footwear had not emerged as a problem. This only arose afterwards when Fitzgerald mentioned it to the media:

> I was moved to reveal the Department of Finance had argued that, because some women had smaller feet than some children, such a distinction should not be made. This argument had tickled my fancy during the pre-budget cabinet discussions, and had stuck in my mind. It also stuck in the minds of the media. My attempt to lighten the occasion had instantly transformed our budget defeat from an issue of food subsidies into one about children's shoes. And, unsurprisingly, Jim Kemmy saw no reason, subsequently, to correct this misinterpretation. Thus are myths created. And, once created, they seem to endure forever.

But Joe Kemmy disagreed with Fitzgerald's perspective:

> Jim was in touch with me the whole time and VAT on children's shoes was definitely an issue from the very start, equal to the food subsidies. Jim fully understood what he was doing.

The fall of the first Fitzgerald coalition was followed by the election of February 1982. Kemmy was returned to the Dáil, certainly boosted by his fame in causing the collapse of the government. During the election, local criticism was voiced by his political opponent, Des O'Malley, then a Fianna Fáil TD. O'Malley was scathing, arguing that although Kemmy was elected as the 'allegedly most out-and-out socialist in the country, but worked as quite the opposite, voting for every single item he was asked to, including things one would not expect a socialist to vote for'.[21]

In the Dáil, the parties vied with each other for support from the non-allied TDs. Charles Haughey canvassed Kemmy for his vote, but the meeting between the two was short and unproductive. According to Joe Kemmy: 'Haughey introduced the discussion by telling Jim about his shared interest in stone, and how Haughey had used local stone on his holiday home on the Blasket Islands – that was a like a red rag to a bull, Jim was distinctly unimpressed.' There was also an offer to Kemmy from Fianna Fáil of the post of Ceann Comhairle, chairman of the Dáil, exempting him from the need for re-election, an offer curtly refused.[22] According to Seamus Harrold: 'Haughey sent Brian Lenihan to Limerick to lobby Jim for his vote, but Jim wasn't having it.' Kemmy voted for Fitzgerald as taoiseach, although Charles Haughey secured the majority vote to form the government, supported by the Workers Party and some other independents. The election of Charles Haughey as taoiseach would have been viewed with particular bitterness by Labour supporters, who would have argued that Kemmy's sole contribution had been to provide an opportunity for the return to power of Fianna Fáil, and perhaps to advance further his own personal profile.

Speaking in the Dáil on the formation of the government, Kemmy said:

> I am not in any way dismayed, terrified or alarmed at the close outcome of this election and I think there will be many more such results in time to come. We must all learn to live dangerously in politics. I am satisfied, however, that this tight situation in the balance of power will bring about greater public accountability by future governments and this is surely a good thing.

The goal of full employment has never been taken seriously and has been considered unrealistic. . . . The first
national aim should be full employment for our people. .
. . As well as the right to work, I have also discussed with
the two candidates the right of people to adequate housing and accommodation. This is a fundamental human
right which is being ignored in our society. It can no longer be ignored because it is totally unacceptable that, at a
time when people are crying out for housing and accommodation, wealthy and influential people should exploit
this human need for personal profit and private gain. It
is also unacceptable that these people should make mil-
lions of pounds profit at the expense of fellow human beings through the mere re-zoning of agricultural land for
building purposes.[23]

Later, during the same Dáil term, Kemmy spoke on other
issues, such as calling for more rigorous control of voting lists:
'In the last election I caught six people impersonating and I
booted them out of the polling booth. I did not go any further
with that, but they ran like rats.'[24] Also, reflecting his urban,
working class perspective, he was especially critical of the
farmer lobby groups:

The farmers have had the best of all worlds for too long
and they see themselves as being somewhat apart from
society and having a right to do as they wish with their
land. . . . There is no point in molly-coddling farmers as
we have done in the past. In modern society they must
pull their weight. . . . There is no reason why farming here
cannot be productive and efficient, but our farming must
surely be the most inefficient in Europe. We have ladled
out money to farmers for decades and they must show
some return for it.[25]

Kemmy's penchant for strong words was not restricted to
the Dáil. In the same year, he issued a sharp rebuke to the

Gardaí. The immediate issue was that, because of cutbacks in public sector pay, crime controls could be withdrawn from some areas in Limerick. In a public statement,[26] Jim Kemmy criticised the Gardaí for this. 'There should be greater sense of duty to the public,' he said. 'Gardaí were selling videos, building bungalows and acting as "bouncers" (private security) for local discos instead of looking after people.' This drew a heated response from the Garda Representative Association, calling on Jim Kemmy to substantiate his claims. A further reaction was from the Association of Garda Sergeants and Inspectors, claiming that the remarks were defamatory and a scurrilous accusation of criminal corruption against the Gardaí. Both organisations urged Jim Kemmy to give any evidence of corruption to the Director of Public Prosecution.[27] Defending his position, Kemmy issued a further and lengthier statement:

'Guarding the Gardaí'
On 26 August 1982, I made a statement in which I criticised certain abuses and malpractices within the Gardaí. It was one of the few occasions in the history of the state that the police force has been so openly criticised by a member of the Dáil . . . some sections of the force could write their own overtime . . . double jobbing . . . political influence all too often plays a part in promotion.

Reaction to my statement was interesting. . . . Garda spokesmen pretended that there was nothing wrong with the force. The almost total and unanimous silence of the politicians was remarkable Indeed, politicians from the three main parties came forward to provide me with further examples of Garda abuse. I received hundreds of letters agreeing with my criticism. I became aware that politicians and police were well aware of what was wrong with the Gardaí. The freemasonry code within the police decreed that members could not speak out in public about such activities.

Almost all politicians have attempted and, in many cases, succeeded in 'fixing' summons and charges against their constituents. So, when a crunch situation emerges between police and public, most politicians have to sing dumb for fear of exposure of their past 'fixing'. The internal politics of the police force is worthy of a special study. The Gardaí are highly politicised and, as the politicians make use of the police, so the police make use of the politicians, especially when it comes to promotion.[28]

Editorials in the media at the time drew attention to the Kemmy allegations and called for an investigation, but felt that the statements were regrettable without evidence. Kemmy had a meeting with the Deputy Commissioner for the Gardaí which was described as 'cordial'. The Deputy Commissioner agreed to investigate Jim Kemmy's allegations. There were no further pronouncements by either side, and matters rested. Seamus Harrold told the author: 'In the Guards controversy Patsy got some nasty phone calls . . . Jim told me he was ashamed by what he saw as some bad behaviour of some Guards, but he couldn't bring it any further.'

But Kemmy's critique of the Gardaí did not stop there. Several years later, in 1994, on the *Questions and Answers* programme in RTÉ, he said that the Gardaí should show good example by enforcing and observing the new drink-driving regulations, drawing a sharp rebuke from the Garda Representative Association as an allegation that the Gardaí were breaking the law. However, this was denied by Kemmy, saying that was not what he meant.[29]

Back in the Dáil, the Haughey government fell with the loss of support from the Workers Party, followed by a general election in November 1982. In this election, Kemmy faced considerable pressure from the local Labour Party, who were targeting his seat. The media[30] at the time reported that Kemmy had received 6,000 first preferences in February 1982 as an independent candidate, and had consolidated the working class vote in the big housing schemes in Southill, Garryowen and Moyross. A contributory factor in Kemmy's showing at the time was that he had brought down the coalition government by voting against their tough budget, a stand that won him support in working class areas. But this success was short-lived. Subsequently, Kemmy failed to enjoy the same high profile he received as a power broker when he 'pulled the rug from under Garret Fitzgerald and plunged the country into a general election'. Labour put forward a candidate, Frank Prendergast, who had a united group of workers behind him. A further issue was the national resurgence of the Labour Party, under their new leader Dick Spring, who was gaining in popularity.

A second negative factor for Kemmy was the Pro-Life Amendment Campaign. This was one of the prominent issues dominating the election, seeking to insert a right to life amendment to the Constitution, with the proposed wording:

> The state acknowledges the right to life of the unborn, and with due regard to the equal right to life of the mother, guarantees in its laws to respect and, so far as practicable, by its laws to defend and vindicate that right.

The proposal had considerable support in principle across the political spectrum. Kemmy, however, was opposed to the referendum, arguing that an absolute prohibition of abortion was not justified, as abortion might be necessary in exceptional circumstances. This was associated with the views of his new emerging party, the Democratic Socialist Party (DSP). Ray Kavanagh told the author:

> The 1982/83 anti-abortion amendment proposal was very controversial. It over-simplified everything but there was a huge steam-roller behind it and the politicians were ter-

rified about this. Jim Kemmy was one of the few people with the courage to oppose it.

Kemmy drew intensive criticisms for this position, including from the influential local media, with the *Limerick Leader* issuing a strident editorial under the title 'The Stench of Death':

> So now we know, Limerick's deputy Jim Kemmy, who likes keeping his cards close to his chest, has at long last shown his Democratic Socialist Party's hand on abortion. They are in favour . . . the party's abortion policy is more than a mere political blunder; it is a horrific assault on a defenceless section of society and must therefore be resisted.[31]

The *Limerick Leader* followed up later with another sharp onslaught on Kemmy's position. On the front page, facing a report where Kemmy argued that the pro-life groups were being narrow and sectarian and that there was no need for a referendum, the *Limerick Leader* published a special 'comment':

> Abortionist Jim Kemmy is hitting below the belt . . . let the people decide which is the better way – the pro-life way or Kemmy's way of death.[32]

Joe Kemmy told the author:

> This was absolutely libellous and the *Leader* retracted it later, but it was awful and did Jim dreadful damage in the election. The whole thing smacked of a conspiracy: there were letters about this in the paper against Jim from people who did not even exist – we checked.

Niall Greene told the author: 'The role of the *Limerick Leader* in the abortion referendum was really nasty stuff, but that is what the freedom of the press is all about.' According to Seamus Harrold:

Jim was railroaded into the abortion controversy. The founding members of the DSP in Dublin went too far in opposing the amendment, that was all right in Dublin but in Limerick it made Jim's position untenable and it was political suicide, there was strong group in the DSP in Dublin vehemently against the amendment, and Jim accepted their vote at a meeting in Dublin, Jim could take the rough with the smooth, once he believed in something he would stick with it.

Seamus Harrold continued:

Brendan Halligan had heard about the DSP policy, we tried to hide it in Limerick, but he sent a journalist to check the DSP policies, saw the opposition to the amendment, then put the hatchet in. There was no hiding with Jim, everything had to be done straight down the line. Jim didn't compromise on situations, he didn't do deals.

This combination of factors proved too much for Kemmy, losing his seat to Labour's Frank Prendergast. Dick Spring explained to the author: 'Those were difficult times, the Labour Party felt that Jim Kemmy was exposed on the abortion issue, and we were certainly not shy in exploiting that.'

Following his failure in the election, Jim Kemmy said[33] that the abortion issue was a major factor in his defeat. He criticised the Catholic Church, the *Limerick Leader*, the Labour Party and Fianna Fáil: 'They all played the abortion card.' Jim Kemmy claimed that sermons dealing with the abortion issue were 'orchestrated' in city churches in the Sunday before the election and he accused the *Limerick Leader* of using scare headlines to give the impression that he was totally in favour of abortion on demand. He stood by his policy that abortion could be justified if the woman's life was endangered, or in case of rape, or where there was congenital deformity of the foetus. Jim Kemmy said that a headline in the *Limerick Lead-*

The 1911 census return of the Kemmy family in Garryowen. The strong family connection with the brick and stonemason trade is evident, with his grandfather (Joseph) and his two uncles (Thomas and Joseph) already stonemasons, and his father (Michael) listed as scholar, soon to be also a stonemason. All worked in Limerick. (National Archives)

The 1911 census return of the Pilkington family in Kilmihil, County Clare. Among 11 children recorded, Jim Kemmy's mother was Elizabeth (Eliza on the form). Their father was described as a general labourer. Almost all the children emigrated – a common experience for labouring rural families at the time. (National Archives)

On the plinth at Dáil Eireann (1990s)
(Limerick Leader)

Launch of *Angela's Ashes* with author Frank McCourt (1996) *(Limerick Leader)*

At the Labour Party annual conference in the 1990s with Dick Spring
(Irish Times)

At the Dáil in the early 1980s with other independent TDs
Joe Sherlock and Noel Browne *(Irish Times)*

With apprentices from the building industry (1970s) (*Limerick Leader*)

Recognizing 300 years of the Plasterers & Slaters Society (1970s) (*Limerick Leader*)

Working with Limerick City Council (1970s) (*Limerick Leader*)

Launch of the *Limerick Socialist* (1972) (Building and Allied Trades Union)

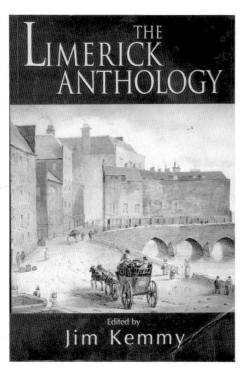

Limerick Anthology (1996) (Limerick City Library*)*

A mayor for all ages

Holes in his shoes! (*Limerick Leader*)

The Limerick City Museum was renamed The Kemmy Municipal Museum in 2000
(www.limerick.ie)

Labour Party TD Jan O'Sullivan TD, who officially unveilled a new portrait of
Jim Kemmy at the Kemmy Business School in October 2008. ALso pictured is Joe
Kemmy, , brother of the late Jim Kemmy (www2.ul.ie)

Chairman of the Labour Party
during the 1990s *(Limerick Leader)*

er on the eve of the election – 'Kemmy backs DSP policy on abortion' – gave the wrong impression. In further justification, Kemmy claimed that his stance was almost identical to that of the Irish Council of Protestant Churches.

However, Brendan Halligan of the *Limerick Leader* told the author:

> It is true that, editorially, in response to Jim's attacks on the pro-life position, I blasted his pro-choice position. Our news coverage, however, was impartial. The electorate were entitled to know where the candidates stood. In the run-up to the election Jim was initially and uncharacteristically reluctant to say where he stood. Eventually, however, he did make a comment, which was published along with comments from other candidates.

Manus O'Riordan told the author:

> In the anti-amendment campaign, we felt it was essential to have a clear policy. Our stance in the DSP was identical to that of the Church of Ireland and the Jewish congregation, but we got very negative press coverage. Frank Prendergast played the 'Catholic card' against Jim.

Joe Wallace of the University of Limerick explained:

> Specifically on the abortion controversy it is interesting that the Irish State has continuously fudged the issue and failed to meet the requirement identified by the Supreme Court to legislate on the issue – something which has now been identified by the European Court of Human Rights. Jim's stance on abortion was typical, emphatic and principled, while it temporarily damaged him politically in the long run, the fact that he was prepared to take such stances worked in his favour – sometimes even among people who did not agree with a specific stance.

Although now out of the Dáil, Kemmy maintained his active political life. He continued in his role as an elected member of Limerick City Council, working also as a trade union official. Seamus Harrold told the author: 'Loosing the election in 1982, we were all devastated, but Jim took it on the chin, but it was like a death in the family for the rest of us.'

According to his secretary, Margaret O'Donoghue, Kemmy had suffered for his opposition to the abortion amendment. Nobody called to Kemmy's office for some time after that. He was not for abortion, said Margert O'Donoghue. But people would say 'there's the man who wanted people to kill the babies'. After the 1982 election loss, Kemmy concentrated on union work and local government. He went back to doing clinics in Moyross and Southill. Jim Kemmy walked everywhere; he never had a car, so people could meet him easily. 'You would get all sorts of complaints and requests, sometimes on a bit of paper or off the back of a beer mat.' People on the train would come up to him with a request for assistance. He would walk into the officials' offices to intervene for people. The local historian Kevin Hannon called him the 'late Jim Kemmy' – he was never on time, reported Margaret O'Donoghue. According to Jan O'Sullivan:

> He worked hard on the ground, held clinics, helped people, stuck with it. Jim Kemmy had a real identity, huge personal relationship with many people, lots of people knew him, he was highly visible.

This substantial supporting network is evident in many comments: 'Jim had two active supporters who drove him everywhere: Liam O'Connor and John Flynn,' reported Joe Kemmy.

Endnotes

1. Verling, 1999.

2. *The Irish Labour Party in Transition* by Michael Gallagher (Manchester University Press, 1982).

3. *Limerick Weekly Echo*, 22 January 1972 (from Joe Kemmy).

4. A radical political outlook that advocates bringing industry and government under the control of the trade unions.

5. *Limerick Leader*, 21 December 1994.

6. Kemmy Collection, UL.

7. *Modern Ireland, 1600-1972*, by R.F. Foster (Penguin, London, 1988).

8. *Limerick Leader*, 12 June 1978.

9. *Limerick Leader*, 18 August 1979.

10. *Twentieth Century Ireland: Nation and State* by Dermot Keogh (Gill and Macmillan, Dublin 1994).

11. Press release, February 1985 (Kemmy Collection, UL).

12. Bourke had gained notoriety in 1966 by helping the Soviet spy George Blake escape from prison in Britain, later moving to Moscow, before subsequently returning to Limerick, and successfully avoiding extradition attempts by the UK authorities.

13. *Limerick Echo*, 20 June 1981.

14. Dáil debates, 7 July 1981.

15. Dáil debates, July 1981.

16. Dáil debates, October 1981.

17. Divorce Action Group, Galway, November, 1981 (Kemmy Collection, UL).

18. Statement on 15 January 1982 by Jim Kemmy setting pre-conditions for support for 1982 budget (Kemmy Collection, UL).

19. *Hiding behind a Face – Fine Gael under Fitzgerald* by Stephen O'Byrnes (Gill and Macmillan, Dublin, 1986).

20. *Irish Times*, 9 September 2000.

21. *Limerick Leader*, 30 January, 1982.

22. Luke Verling, 1999.

23. Dáil debates, 9 March 1982.

24. Dáil debates, 29 April 1982.

25. Dáil debates, 7 July 1982.

26. *Evening Press*, 24 August 1982 (Kemmy Collection, UL).

27. *Irish Times*, 27 August 1982 (Kemmy Collection, UL).

28. Statement by Jim Kemmy, 29 August 1982 (Kemmy Collection, UL).

29. *Limerick Leader*, 17 December 1994.

30. *Cork Evening Echo*, 20 November 1982 (Kemmy Collection, UL).

31. *Limerick Leader*, 10 April 1982.

32. *Limerick Leader*, 2 October 1982.

33. *Irish Times*, 26 November 1982 (Kemmy Collection, UL).

3

Democratic Socialist Party

Jim Kemmy's energies were now being directed towards the development of a new political party, the Democratic Socialist Party, or DSP for short.[1] A note at the time summarised the aims of the new DSP:

> Formation of a party which will be socialist, secularist, post-nationalist and democratic. Such a party should have a programme which includes a basic commitment to the long-term goal of a socialist society, as well as outlining a number of broad policy goals. The basic platform should contain neither a detailed blueprint of long term, nor detailed policies on all current issues. The party should be open to those who agree with the basic platform, including Marxist and non-Marxist socialists.[2]

During 1981, after his first election to the Dáil, Kemmy had discussions with individuals interested in the possibilities of setting up a new socialist grouping to emulate in other parts of the country what Kemmy had achieved in Limerick. Discussions were with the Socialist Party, Irish Communist Organisation, individual members of the Labour Party, Socialists against Nationalism and others. It was agreed that there was enough common ground for a new democratic socialist party. By the end of 1981, a meeting in Limerick noted that as many as 30 people in Dublin were involved in discussion, with potential for a national party focused on Dublin, Cork and Limerick. But there also a feeling at that meeting that the DSP could cost Kemmy votes, with a possible weakening of his support as a purely local and independent representative. However, on balance, it was agreed that having a party base would increase the opportunity for a national breakthrough, with the strength of a wider national movement. The aim, the participants felt, should be a broad-based liberal socialist party to fill the vacuum left by the Labour Party's failure to provide leadership for Irish workers.

Manus O'Riordan explained:

> Following Jim Kemmy's election in 1981, the 'Two Nations' group re-formed themselves into 'Socialists against Nationalism'. By that time, Kemmy felt there was a basis for a general socialist alliance, beyond the specific issues of Northern Ireland. Many members of BICO moved over to join the new party of Kemmy, with Martin McGarry becoming general secretary, he was a critical supporter of Jim Kemmy. We collaborated with Jim Kemmy as an individual who was not in BICO; he never joined. He obviously felt the Communist philosophy was not for him – we frequently gave him invitations to join, but he probably felt he would lose support by being too close to BICO. BICO acknowledged Jim Kemmy as a key socialist influence and campaigned for him in '77. We saw his group as very important in promoting education about socialism in Limerick, and in encouraging debates about the issues.

The Party Platform of November 1981 set out the guiding principles:

- The DSP aims to build a socialist society, in which the creation and distribution of wealth will be under democratic public control, and in which the right to work will be guaranteed to all.

- A democratic society in which workers will have a greater say in running their workplaces.

- The political system of parliamentary democracy provides the best framework towards a democratic socialist society.

- DSP seeks to develop a secular society. Religious belief should not be enshrined in law and religious organisations should not control public institutions. In particular, the party will campaign against the undemocratic social power of the Catholic Church.

- DSP rejects the claim by the Republic of Ireland to jurisdiction over Northern Ireland . . . the party accepts the right of the majority in Northern Ireland to live in a state of their own choosing.

- The DSP recognises that Irish workers have a common interest with workers elsewhere in ending oppression.

- The DSP seeks a society where all citizens are treated equally.

Kemmy's trade union background was evident in the systematic and methodical approach taken to structuring the DSP. The constitution of the new party had no less than 102 sections – rules, procedures, role of branches, party conferences, standing orders. Guidelines were issued on the formation of local branches. Suggestions for branch activities included several practical points: know the physical layout of your own area, know your people (especially associations and groups), identify the local problems like unemployment and housing, create public debate locally, promote local publicity, fund raising, political clinics, encourage branch education through debate on political issues, local recruitment to the DSP.

In March 1982, a press statement was issued on the launch of the DSP:

> In the past two decades, the Republic has changed from being primarily a rural-based society to an urban-based one. The majority of our population now live not in the country but in large towns and cities. This has led to a re-assessment of values and a re-defining of interests. The DSP will reflect and represent this change.
>
> The new party is socialist, secularist and post-nationalist. It is a pure socialist party in that it has no ties, past or present, with the republican or nationalist traditions. It stands for a secular society, which will uphold the individual's right to practise and proclaim the religion of his choice but will oppose control of publicly-funded bodies by the churches.
>
> The DSP is post-nationalist in that it believes that nationalism has played far too long an excessively important role in society and that the nationalist catch-cries and shibboleths have been used to blind people to their real interests and the interests of society.

Following the February 1982 election, an abortive attempt was initiated by Jim Kemmy to negotiate an alliance of the left with some other TDs – Tony Gregory and three from the Workers Party – but this came to nothing as the Workers Party backed Charles Haughey instead.

Although the November 1982 elections saw the loss of Jim Kemmy's seat, with no wins for the DSP, Kemmy was as enthusiastic as ever. Speaking in February 1983, he said:

> We have come together at a crucial time in the history of our state. Our people are confronted with unprecedented problems and difficulties. Almost 200,000 people are unemployed. We are a society in crisis sixty-one years af-

ter self-governance, the ruling political parties have run the ship of state on the rocks and they are bankrupt of ideas about how to get it back on course. . . . The fact that our party suffered a defeat in the recent general election through the loss of a Dáil seat has not in any way discouraged us. Indeed, this defeat has merely steeled our determination not only to win back this seat but to continue to confront the forces of reaction not only in Limerick but everywhere we find them.

The 1984 European elections were contested, although unsuccessfully, by John De Courcy Ireland for the DSP, with this manifesto:

Devoid of humanity, brotherhood or community, international business interests are prepared to sacrifice everything to the single goal of profit. The world market they have structured for themselves is grossly unbalanced and wasteful of the world's resources . . . yet in western Europe there exists vast potential – the economic, technological and political means are there for organising a positive response to the crisis and negotiating a new world economic system based on co-operation which would restore progress and end the stagnation of productive forces.

The DSP was thus staunchly pro-Europe, seeing the EU as the vehicle for a strong worker response to the dominance of the international business interests.

During 1983-84, the DSP issued a series of policy papers, setting out its position on several national controversies: Church and State, taxation, employment, women's rights, anti-amendment on abortion, drug abuse, building land and Northern Ireland. The papers were coherent and well-written, reflecting the thinking of the articulate group of activists that Kemmy had drawn around himself.

On Church and State, the DSP argued for full separation:

> We are not opposed to religion: rather we view it as a private matter between the individual and his/her church, if he/she has one. We recognise the rights of individuals, church and religious associations to hold and proclaim their various views; we oppose the enshrining of religious beliefs in law. In particular we believe that religious institutions should not control public institutions. Democratic control of such institutions and public accountability for public funds: these are the keystones for policy in this area.

On specifics, the calls by DSP were for: democratic management of all schools; remove the constitutional ban on divorce legislation; allow for the sale of contraceptives to all who need them, with a comprehensive system of family planning advice; in health, there should be full accountability of public funds, and an end to the situation of church-owned voluntary hospitals being treated as 'a state within a state'.

The DSP argued that inequalities of the taxation system represented one of the most urgent economic grievances facing the working class of the republic. The PAYE sector was overtaxed through fixed income bands; capital taxation was absurdly low and getting lower; tax evasion was exceptionally high; and there was a huge imbalance in the distribution of the tax burden between town and country. Measures proposed were to reduce tax evasion and tax avoidance, introduce a resource tax on agriculture and raise both capital taxation and corporation tax.

Unemployment was reported by DSP to be the most serious social problem in the country, one that could not be resolved without some fundamental changes in Ireland's approach to economic policy. DSP acknowledged the usefulness of much that has been done in the past to increase employ-

ment. Welcome though this may be, it had not proved suffi-
cient, claimed the DSP. The DSP was wholeheartedly committed to the principle of full employment.

> We believe that its achievement is best approached in
> the context of a planned economy with economic priori-
> ties and broad lines of development being worked out by
> the main participants in the economy – the government,
> unions and representatives of industry. We believe also
> that the main trust of economic development and the
> main burden of job creation will be taken by a productive
> industrial sector serviced and financed by various state
> institutions and accountable in turn for its performance
> to the state.

Specific DSP proposals were: a National Enterprise Agency
to identify, research and develop products for manufacture;
a state development corporation as a holding company for
commercial state enterprises; and a special agency to promote
worker co-operative enterprises.

On women's rights, DSP argued that sexual equality meant
a new deal for both women and men. The urgent need was for
political commitment for women's rights. There was a need
for reorganisation of child-rearing as the responsibility of
both parents and society in general. For equal pay, legislation
was not enough – trade unions should give positive encouragement to women to organise themselves. DSP accepted that
in the short term women would be mainly involved in rear-
ing children in the home. State support should be through
children's allowances. The educational system should equip
girls for long-term participation in the labour force in terms
of equality with men. The DSP recommended abolition of
the narrow legal definition of the family in terms of marriage
alone.

DSP reported that it was the only political party to affiliate to the anti-amendment campaign, and was opposed to the insertion of the 'right to life' clause in the constitution.

> Little notice has been taken of the fact that all religious groupings other than the Catholic Church opposed the inclusion of such a clause in the constitution. In a country where conservative estimates number ten women a day travelling to England for abortion, we must admit that we have an abortion problem and that this amendment will make no difference to the situation.

DSP claimed to be the only party to have discussed the problem of abortion openly and honestly. DSP also argued that they were the only party to have formulated a policy on which it states that it considers abortion to be a solution to the terrible problems of severe abnormality of the foetus, serious threat to the mother's life, or pregnancy resulting from rape or incest.

Drug abuse was viewed as a growing problem, with Irish urban centres, particularly Dublin, seeing a massive increase in addiction to opiate-style drugs, mainly heroin. This development occurred alongside an alarming ongoing increase in the consumption of tranquillisers and sedatives, and despite a consistently severe alcoholism problem. DSP proposed a range of responses at community level, at the level of coordinated treatment and rehabilitation, within the prison system, within the education system and within the prescribing medical profession.

On building land, DSP argued that it was imperative that steps were taken to curb land speculation and all the attendant anti-social consequences. The difference in price which existed between agricultural and building land – almost tenfold – was unjustifiable. The speculative profits which could be made from dealing in land were correspondingly excessive, bearing no relation to any incentive that might be required to release land for building purposes.

The conflict in Northern Ireland presented a particularly acute problem for democratic society, according to the DSP. What was at issue were two contending rights to national self-determination – those of the unionists and those of the nationalists in Northern Ireland. DSP supported the rights of Ulster unionists to remain within the UK outside a unitary Irish state; DSP recognised the Irish national identity of the nationalist population and would support any potential settlement based on the recognition which did not undermine the rights of unionists. DSP argued that the Republic should abandon its undemocratic claim over the unionist population, and encouraged the nationalist population to seek a means of national fulfilment which did not disregard the rights of unionists. DSP also called for extradition of suspected terrorists from the Republic to Northern Ireland, in cases of specific offences coming under the European Convention on the Suppression of Terrorism.

In an undated speech around this time, Jim Kemmy summed up their approach: 'The only democratic policy is full recognition of the right of the majority in Northern Ireland to live in a state of their own choosing; and full recognition of the minority's entitlement to full civil and legal rights.'

Niall Greene told the author:

> The DSP would have drawn much of their thinking about the 'Two Nations Theory' from the British and Irish Communist Party (BICO) and especially from their front organisation the Campaign for the Democratic Resolution of the National Question. The BICO was a break-away group from the main Communist Party and advocated the idea that the Northern Ireland Protestants were a separate nation in their own right and entitled, if that was what they wished, to have their own autonomous state, provid-

ed it fully respected the human rights of other citizens in its jurisdiction. Although not formally linked to BICO, Jim and the DSP were very much influenced by this thinking.

A series of local DSP branches were established: Dublin North Central, Dublin West, Limerick, Dun Laoghaire, Blackrock and Cork. Much of the work over 1982–86 focused on setting up the machinery of the new political party. DSP thus embraced a substantial arena with their own specific approach to policy, but not without internal tensions. According to Manus O'Riordan:

There were a lot of 'cultural' differences between the Dublin and Limerick members of the DSP. For example, the Dublin members would be all against blood sports, but for Jim, with coursing so popular in Limerick, that was definitely a 'no-go' area.

Seamus Harrold reported:

The crowd in the DSP were all genuine people, no skulduggery, but it was heavy going whenever the elections were on, every evening, five nights a week out between 7.00 pm and 10.00 pm, you could never have any family life at all with that.

The results of the local elections in 1985 showed that the DSP was well established in Limerick. However, the election results in Dublin were disappointing, with several difficulties: the DSP was seen to lack recognition as a distinct party outside Limerick; Dublin DSP candidates were perceived by the public as independents, rather than party representatives. According to Jan O'Sullivan:

Jim Kemmy wanted to leave some legacy, leave something to young people. He found the Labour Party too conservative, he wanted to be part of a movement, wanted to be in a party, wanted to gather people around himself. However, the DSP was all very intellectual, very high level of debate, all 'chiefs and no Indians', lots of policy papers. They had top-level political thinkers, but we didn't have troops on the ground.

Dan Miller told the author:

The DSP had great people who could intellectualise everything, but we never won any seats. We were going nowhere with DSP, but Jim knew he had to bring people with him, with their heads held high, he wanted to create a genuine left/right divide in Irish politics.

In 1987, the second Fitzgerald coalition collapsed, to be replaced in the ensuing election by a minority government led by Charles Haughey. Jim Kemmy was re-elected to the Dáil, although the only member of the DSP to win a seat. Seamus Harrold explained:

We won the seat in 1987, result of very hard work on the ground, people began to realise Jim had been 'shafted' in 1982. Dublin supporters came down to help out, they would sleep on the floor in Patsy's and Joe's house, they would really swell the ranks. The Dublin canvassers would join the group going round, but would not talk too much on the doorstep, that was done by the Limerick supporters.

No other DSP candidate was successful. This poor showing of the DSP in this election, as well as the disappointing outcomes of the local and European elections, confirmed that the new party had little future as a separate political entity. A further factor had been the formation of the Progressive Democrats in 1985, led by Des O'Malley. Kemmy viewed this as a right-wing group, presenting the Left with a strong challenge. This was reflected in a speech by Kemmy at the time:

Our country and our people are now at an unprecedented crisis since the state was founded sixty-five years ago. Sadly for us as socialists the economic and political response to this crisis has not come from the left but from the right. The response from the left to the crisis has been sluggish and uncoordinated. The fragmentation and division among the Irish socialist parties has contributed to this situation. We need to build a strong and united socialist movement in this country. We must face the fact that there is not room for three left-wing parties (Labour, Workers Party and DSP) in the country.[3]

In April 1986, Jim Kemmy had written as president of the DSP to the leader of the Labour Party, Dick Spring, to the Workers Party and to the two independents, Noel Browne and Tony Gregory to 'suggest a meeting to explore common ground on the Left in the lead-up to the next general election'. In May 1988, the Workers Party (Pronsias De Rossa) and Jim Kemmy met to discuss possible areas of cooperation, and issued a joint statement: 'In the light of the right-wing consensus among the majority of the Dáil, it was essential that the socialist parties should cooperate . . .'

Ray Kavanagh was General Secretary of the Labour Party at the time. In a history[4] of the party covering this period, Kavanagh recounted the events, explaining how his strategy was to strengthen the Labour Party in opposition, positioning it as a party that could enter government with a mandate. In 1986, Ray Kavanagh had become general secretary of the Labour Party, telling the author he always had the height of admiration for Kemmy:

Jim Kemmy had courage always on the side of the underdog, the Irish system of his time was very monolithic, centrally dominated by the Catholic Church, Kemmy was able to stand out against all of this, in a very gentle way, without recrimination.

In Limerick, Kavanagh's approach was to encourage the incorporation of Jim Kemmy and the DSP into the Labour Party. Visiting the local organisation there, he gauged the depths of bitterness in their feelings. According to Kavanagh, there was an enormous chasm to be bridged. The fact that Kemmy was then a TD only made matters more challenging. Nevertheless, he felt he was dealing with pragmatists who would accept a respectful compromise if it were presented properly – but it would take time. The gulf was painfully demonstrated to Kavanagh in 1987 when he travelled to Limerick. He broached the subject of a union with the DSP, but the proposal was denounced in emphatic and free-flowing rhetoric by local Labour interests. Not one person out of the 40 attending the meeting supported his suggestion.

Preparing for the general election in 1989, Kavanagh returned to Limerick. He wanted to merge the party there with the DSP, but was nowhere near agreement. He argued that, to hold on to Labour's negotiating strength, Labour had to contest the election, though everybody knew that Jim Kemmy held the left-wing seat and there was not a second one available. The Labour Party in Limerick was still very hostile to a merger with the DSP. He brought up the subject, as he usually did at meetings in Limerick, to get people used to the idea. 'My relatives are buried in the graveyard over there,' one delegate roared. 'If Jim Kemmy returned to the Labour party, their bones would rattle.'

Kavanagh had been assiduously attending to every problem that might arise in the case of a merger between Labour and the DSP. A very important part of this work was building strong personal bonds between both organisations and Kavanagh himself. This involved scores of trips to Limerick in the period 1987-90, and marked the beginning of many friendships, in particular with Jim Kemmy. Ray Kavanagh explained to the author how he worked to bring Jim Kemmy into the Labour Party. Ray Kavanagh and Kemmy were on the same agenda, he reported. In the end, the ultimate merger between the Labour Party and the DSP worked well, achieved without rancour or recrimination and, most important, no members were lost on either side, according to Kavanagh: 'The key was to reassure both sides that they were not going to be bullied. The problem with any merger is not to allow one side to be too dominant.'

Dick Spring explained to the author that there were several issues that needed to be confronted in this delicate process:

> Time is a great healer, it was clear that Jim Kemmy was in possession of the seat in Limerick, and it was obvious that a rapprochement was the order of the day. Kemmy was adamant that he was not just an independent TD. He felt he had an organisation behind him, but it was really a Jim Kemmy movement, left-wing and liberal. Ray Kavanagh had to watch his back carefully – there were many old Labour families, there was a lot of bitterness between Kemmy and old Labour. Jim Kemmy was not rushing to join the Labour Party – he was not comfortable about the Labour Party stance on social issues. Kemmy was certainly very close to Labour on economic issues, but, overall, he was extremely wary about going back to the Labour Party. Ray Kavanagh had to bring his people with him. I would not have had the patience that Ray had with the DSP, but Ray was able to bring them along.

Over time, the traditionalist Labour group in Limerick saw the merit of re-grouping. Following meetings between both groups, led by Niamh Breathnach, chairperson of the party, agreement on merger was secured. Winning the agreement of the existing Labour Party in Limerick was based on their being given fair access to contest the forthcoming local elections. The attitude of the former TD, Frank Prendergast, was remarkable, according to Kavanagh. The agreement held little for him, yet Prendergast supported it wholeheartedly in the interests of Labour.

In June 1989, the Labour Party national conference agreed a cooperation of the Left, acknowledging that DSP was an ally of the Labour Party. The aim was to mobilise an alliance against the right-wing economic consensus in the Dáil.

Manus O'Riordan told the author about these events:

> Later in the 1980s, we could all see there was no future for the DSP as a distinct element in the Irish political system. In any event, the Labour Party had come much closer to Jim's position, specifically in relation to Northern Ireland, so re-joining the Labour party was inevitable, only a matter of time. Almost all the DSP, about 90%, followed Kemmy into the Labour Party.

Endnotes

1. All documentary sources on the DSP are from the Kemmy Collection (UL).

2. Circular on the establishment of the DSP, November 1981 (Kemmy Collection, UL).

3. Address by Jim Kemmy to Labour Youth Summer camp, August 1987 (Kemmy Collection, UL).

4. *Spring, Summer and Fall – the Rise and Fall of the Labour Party, 1986-99* by Ray Kavanagh, Blackwater Press, Dublin, 2001.

4

The Labour Party
in the 1990s

The 'merger' ceremony took place in Dublin on May Day 1990, with the small room in Buswells Hotel crowded for the occasion. Many DSP members had travelled from Limerick and from around the country to join with the press to fill the room. Dick Spring, according to Kavanagh, was in bad form – 'where's the document?' was all he said during the event. Afterwards, the few Labour people who remained mixed with their new comrades. The merger gave the party a new TD in Jim Kemmy and a new councillor in Jan O'Sullivan. The bitterness that had existed between the two parties now evaporated. 'Kemmy joined the Labour Party seamlessly, people in the parliamentary party welcomed him, he had a substantial following all over the country,' said Ray Kavanagh. Kemmy worked to bring the two sides together. For example, in the subsequent 1991 local elections, he brought in candidates from the mainstream Labour Party onto the 'ticket' in Limerick, and promoted unity between the two sides, according to Ray Kavanagh. This was echoed by Niall Greene, telling the author:

The merger in 1990 went very smoothly. We were unsure if the Kemmy and anti-Kemmy factions in Limerick would come together but there was no problem. The enmities disappeared and the merger became seamless very quickly, once the organisational split was removed, people cooperated in a fresh spirit. Joe Kemmy shortly after the merger became chair of the Constituency Council.

However, in spite of such positive comments, there were still some dissenting views. The media[1] later reported:

The marriage was not welcomed by all the Labour brethren in Limerick, one of whom told the *Irish Times* that 'the Labour Party in Dublin has no idea of the cuckoo they are trying to restore to the nest' – a rather incongruous metaphor to use about the heavily built former stonemason.

Furthermore, the relationship between Kemmy and Spring would continue to be problematical. According to Ray Kavanagh, Spring demonstrated reservations towards Kemmy in 1990.

There could have been a lot of reasons for this. Maybe Spring felt threatened by Jim Kemmy: elder socialist, big profile, as well known as Spring with a strong national image. But also Spring was trying to unify the Labour Party at that time, with many different strands and opinions, a lot of potential divisions, so Spring had to tread carefully, so maybe Spring felt unsure about Kemmy, not knowing on whose side would Kemmy be, and was not certain how to fit him into all this. For whatever reason, Spring certainly kept his distance from Kemmy.

But Dick Spring gave the author a different view:

Personally, I felt I had a solid relationship with Jim Kemmy. We were probably streets apart in one sense. I was

Trinity-educated, a barrister, while Jim was a tradesman. But there were lots of things that bridged the gap and brought us together. On a day-to-day basis we worked very well as a team. I would often go to Limerick to open events for Jim Kemmy.

Ray Kavanagh reported how he had a close friendship with Jim Kemmy, maintaining continuous contact with him, with long conversations on every political topic:

I became very conscious of how Jim Kemmy, while always being surrounded by people, might be very much on his own. TDs are lonely people, they have very few friendships among them, and they are very isolated from each other.

This was echoed by Seamus Harrold:

Jim loved the local scene. Being a TD in the Dáil was really a distraction. He would go up and down on the train every day rather than stay overnight in Dublin. He was always happiest arriving back in Limerick in the evenings. The Dáil can be a very lonely place.

Ray Kavanagh also reported also that Kemmy's lifestyle was none too healthy:

Jim was overweight, often living out of fish-and-chips, other times eating too much of the wrong diet. One anecdote was of a meeting of building trade unions in Limerick, breaking for lunch. Much to everyone's amazement Jim had two substantial main courses at lunch. Afterwards there were ample helpings of dessert in which Jim fully participated. When tea was served he took a box of hermesetas from his pocket and tipped two into his teacup. 'I have to watch my weight nowadays,' he explained to his astonished fellow diners!

Back in the Dáil, Kemmy was active with several interventions reflecting the range of his interests in diverse areas such as Europe, extradition, planning, health and safety, the university and coalition governments.

On Europe, his attitude was:

> . . . guided by a recognition of our common European tradition of democracy, liberty and human rights, in general, especially those of ordinary working people . . . strengthen the socialist influence in Europe. . . . We have plenty of little islanders who see our country as God's gift to Europe. These people want to have their loaf and eat it at the same time. This issue has also flushed out the kind of introverted nationalism which has for so long retarded the progress of our country. Let us learn from the example of Europe. Great traditional enemies in European history such as France, Germany and England have fought many wars but have buried their long and bitter differences and have come together in close political unity. This is a natural and logical development but some people want us as a country to stand aside from these developments and this unity.[2]

Kemmy's support for Europe thus grew naturally from his socialism and anti-nationalism, seeing Europe as an antidote to local parochialism and a boost to workers' rights and workers' interests.

On extradition, Kemmy criticised what he saw to be excessive protection by the courts for republicans, while conventional criminals were extradited regularly:

> I believe everybody should be equal in the eyes of the law, but apparently we have one set of legal rules and regulations for so-called ordinary criminals who have been extradited from this country in the past 22 years without too much fuss or too many debates in this House about them while they were fitted up with evidence from the police

force and elsewhere. Police forces have been known to fit up people with evidence when they had difficulty in proving cases. . . . Is there one set of laws for people who are accused of being terrorists – and are terrorists who plant bombs and perhaps shoot people – and another set of rules for ordinary people who are criminals?[3]

Kemmy's views here were again strongly anti-nationalist, calling for effective enforcement of the law against republicans.

On planning, Kemmy argued for stronger planning from a socialist perspective:

In recent years we have had planning by default, by fear, by cowardice and under the threat of powerful influential people who were out to exploit loopholes in our planning laws. They were not doing that in the interest of the common good or good planning but in the interest of greed and profit. Our cities and towns must, therefore, be protected.[4]

Kemmy's criticism of weaknesses in the planning system reflected his strong views on the need for more assertive policies for protection of the environment and control of development. The stonemason came out here too:

There is no reason whatsoever that we cannot have good functional buildings and good design. It is a myth to say that architects are in the hands of their clients, that they cannot do very much themselves and are more or less prisoners or captives. There is no reason we cannot have good design, good building, good materials and good workmanship combined in any building. . . . We should use more of our natural materials in building work, such as stone which is a most natural material and which has been used for hundreds of thousands of years.

On health and safety, his construction and union experience was evident:

> As somebody who worked in the building industry for about 30 years I am quite familiar with the breaches of safety regulations and I am very concerned about this matter. At a time of economic recession and increased competition in business, safety regulations are often ignored. Cutting corners and taking chances often become, sadly, the order of the day. . . . When a garda or a soldier is killed in the course of his duty his death is given front page headlines and widespread publicity in the media and rightly so because the death of any person in the course of his or her duty is something that should be given attention by the public and the media. However, when a worker is killed during the course of his work his death does not command the same amount of publicity. Indeed, the news of the death of a worker in those circumstances is often tucked away in a paragraph on an inside page of a newspaper.[5]

These comments about health and safety would have reflected the concerns of the time, forcefully expressed by Kemmy in his typical robust and strident manner.

Welcoming the establishment of the University of Limerick, Kemmy's background in construction combined with his virulent anti-nationalism:

> The choice of location of Plassey House, beside the River Shannon, was an ideal and excellent location. . . . We are fortunate that Plassey House was not burned down by some of our so-called patriots who burned down Mountshannon House, the Hermitage at Castleconnell and, indeed, many other fine houses in County Limerick close to Plassey.[6]

In 1989, a new coalition government was formed by Fianna Fáil and the Progressive Democrats. Established in 1985, the Progressive Democrats had represented a group that split away from Fianna Fáil, securing strong results in subsequent elections, and joining Fianna Fáil as a minority partner in a new government. In this instance, Kemmy acknowledged the need for coalition governments, taking examples from Europe:

> We can learn from other countries on the European continent where coalitions are the common denominators. They are the norm in governments in those countries. Since World War II almost every European country, apart from Great Britain, had coalition governments, many of which have worked well. They have had vigorous coalition governments, vigorous opposition parties in which . . . the Left have played a role. There is no good reason why Ireland should be different from any of those European countries.[7]

In a swipe at local Fianna Fáil opponents to the new coalition, he exclaimed:

> What surprises and mystifies me is the reaction of some Fianna Fáil grassroots people. . . . How can people who at local level make all sorts of convoluted arrangements to get power for themselves and offices of chairman of the county council or mayor of the city or the urban area point the finger at Members in this House and say that what they are doing is wrong and what they themselves are doing is right? You cannot play Mighty Mouse in your own constituency and behave in this House like a church mouse.[8]

Ray Kavanagh describes how the colourful character of Jim Kemmy was a dominant feature of the time, impacting on other people with his forceful personality and direct talk, illustrated by two incidents.

In 1990, Mary Robinson was nominated by the Labour Party as their candidate for presidency. On her first public meeting in Limerick, Jim Kemmy gave her advice about clothes. According to Ray Kavanagh, Mary was a good-looking woman and always dressed modestly rather than in high fashion. Left-wing women were all a bit inclined to be a bit dowdy, said Kavanagh. Kemmy, however, was totally scattered about his dress sense. He was absent-minded – sometimes he would leave the house with his shoe laces untied. Patsy Harrold, his friend, and Margaret O'Donoghue, his secretary, did what they could but it was an uphill struggle.

> As often as not, Jim had a bit of his enormous belly sticking out from his open shirt or some food from a recent meal attached to some part of his attire.

But this did not stop him lecturing Mary Robinson, the bluestocking Trinity professor, about her dress sense. He sat her down after the lunch and said to her in his gruff voice: 'Now, Mary, if you want to win this one you'll have to tidy up your act a bit.' Kemmy boasted to Kavanagh about this after the campaign, claiming credit for the transformation in Mary Robinson's appearance. The 1990 presidential campaign provided a major validation for Jim Kemmy within the party, Ray Kavanagh told the author: 'Kemmy really "starred" in the presidential campaign of Mary Robinson – he had a long association with Mary Robinson over the previous years and gave major leadership to her campaign.'

The death of Jimmy Tully, Minister for Local Government, 1973-77, in 1992 was one of Ray Kavanagh's first encounters with what he called Jim Kemmy's 'rigid honesty'. At a meeting of the Parliamentary Labour Party, tributes were given by all speakers about Tully's contribution. Then Jim Kemmy spoke. He mentioned that Jimmy Tully had been deeply conservative on religious and social matters. He said that he had seen him through the eyes of a young man in the sixties and seventies and found him to be very difficult. He did, however, appreciate his practical nature when dealing with the departments for which he was minister. There was a great silence in the room. Kavanagh reported that Jimmy Tully, the harsh and practical realist that he was, would probably have preferred Jim Kemmy's blunt, almost puritan honesty.

The year 1992 also saw the fall from office of Charles Haughey, and his replacement as taoiseach by Albert Reynolds. Elections in November 1992 resulted in a major swing to the Labour Party, led by Dick Spring, with an increase in Labour seats from 15 to 33.

Negotiations commenced between Labour and Fianna Fáil about a new government. However, according to Kavanagh, Dick Spring became isolated from others in the party. The limited socialising in which he had engaged now stopped almost completely. The neurotically secret nature of negotiations was beginning to have a serious effect on the solidarity of the party, reported Kavanagh, writing that Jim Kemmy, perhaps the clearest minded of them all, was 'left to rot in Limerick'. It seemed as if Dick Spring and his political advisor Fergus Finlay intended to do it all by themselves, with others in assisting roles. This attempt at centralisation was to have the most extraordinary consequences, according to Kavanagh.

Jim Kemmy was unhappy about the proposed coalition with Fianna Fáil: 'You are supping with the devil,' he told Dick Spring, 'Fianna Fáil is the party of jobbery, corruption and land speculation.'

Spring's announcement of his cabinet appointments did not include Jim Kemmy. According to Kavanagh, Kemmy felt hurt and tricked at being omitted from ministerial appointment. The *Irish Times* had asked his secretary, Margaret

O'Donoghue, for his biography, acting, he thought, on information from a Labour source. He then realised his name had been omitted from the ministerial list and believed he had been 'set up' by Fergus Finlay, who denied it. Kemmy, as previous leader of the DSP before the merger with Labour, had expected an appointment. Shock waves were felt throughout the party at the decision. Jim Kemmy, who had been leader of his own small party, was not even offered a junior position. Jim Kemmy was deeply wounded at his exclusion. He believed that this outcome was as humiliating as it was inexplicable, reported Kavanagh.

Dick Spring wrote to Kemmy explaining his exclusion from the cabinet:

> I am particularly sorry that it was not possible for me to include your name on this occasion, particularly in view of the large contribution that you made to the recent general election result. These decisions are never easy, and I feel it was fundamentally important to include a strong representation from both the new and the outgoing members of the Dáil

To which Kemmy responded:

> I am philosophical about my exclusion from these appointments. I have been a political activist for 30 years and am well used to the ups and downs of political life . . . the process of formation of the government, amongst other things, served to further my political education. I learnt a good deal about the artistry in which my name was dangled before the media prior to the formation of the government.

Attracting this reply from Spring:

> I have to state most emphatically that neither I nor Fergus Finlay, nor anyone on my staff that I am aware of, had any

hand, act or part in 'dangling' your name before the media prior to the formation of government . . . to engage in such practices would indeed have been very unwise and inconsiderate. I can only ask you to accept my bona fides in this matter. You will appreciate that many friendships and loyalties are temporarily disturbed in the context of these appointments.[9]

Fergus Finlay subsequently defended his position in a later book.[10]

One of Finlay's jobs during the negotiations was to give regular briefings to the political correspondents about progress. The one area where he could not help them, but it came up most days, was the identity of the likely Labour ministers. Finlay claimed that he was not able to help them, and he did not know the names anyway. One name that was regularly floated was that of Jim Kemmy. It was logical because he was something of an icon for the Left, according to Finlay. It was, Finlay believed, conceived by journalists analysing possibilities and probabilities, and quickly developed by the well-oiled Leinster House rumour machine. Jim Kemmy, however, believed that Finlay had floated his name, even though that was untrue. The name of Jim Kemmy, and others, just added to the intrigue surrounding the end of the negotiations, according to Fergus Finlay.

Finlay said he was to discover afterwards that Jim Kemmy desperately wanted to become a minister. When his name appeared on print and in the newspapers, he thought he had secured a job, and never approached Dick Spring to make a case for himself. Finlay reported that he did not know whether Spring would have changed his mind about the team he had put together if Kemmy had approached him. 'Jim Kemmy did not lobby for the post of Minister. That would have been his character, you stood on your record,' said Jan O'Sullivan.

The bottom line, according to Finlay, was that Jim Kemmy came to believe that Finlay had put his name about as part of a 'Machiavellian plot' to undermine his candidacy, and Finlay believed Kemmy never forgave him for it. It contributed also to a frosty relationship between Kemmy and Dick Spring that lasted a long time. While it never undermined Jim Kemmy's loyalty to the party, it gave him occasional pleasure to be slightly mischievous over the following difficult years, reported Fergus Finlay.

Publicly, Kemmy accepted the decision: 'I am not personally hurt or upset or disappointed. You get used to these things in life. I was pleased that I was in contention at all, but it is no good crying over spilt milk.' But Jim Kemmy also warned that he would be a large and relatively loose cannon on the bank benches of government. 'We are all let out in the cold sometimes. I am not at all disgusted. I am too battle-scared for that. This is the nature of politics.'[11]

Dick Spring explained to the author:

> Somebody put it into the media that Jim Kemmy might be appointed to cabinet. It was not me, I would never expose somebody like that. I knew Jim felt very sore that his name was in the public domain. Jim was a big man, but he did carry the hurt, but it was not my making, and I tried to put it behind us as soon as possible. In making the appointments, I had to make sure that all the different factions in the Labour Party were represented. The appointments needed to be spread around the different groups in the Labour Party, you never satisfy everybody. Jim Kemmy would have been considered in that context, but the appointments were about policies and factions, not individuals.

The controversy continued, shared by others who were disappointed with Spring's cabinet decisions:

With some of the twenty-two disappointed people who believed they had been let down by Spring . . . there were forebodings of trouble. Ruffled feathers were not assuaged by the appointment of Jim Kemmy as party chairman. . . . There were rancorous meetings of the parliamentary party while Jim Kemmy and other TDs gave interviews complaining at the direction of government policy. At party meetings, Kemmy expressed his deep annoyance at the way his name and those of other people had been floated in the media as possible ministers. He told colleagues he regarded this as part of an Orwellian disinformation campaign by certain people in the party. . . . Spring suddenly found himself under pressure at party meetings. . . . Jim Kemmy was still annoyed and became a feature of the nightly television news bulletins speaking on the plinth of Leinster House to Charlie Bird of RTÉ.[12]

But Kemmy reported that his appointment as Chairman of the Labour Party was not connected with the controversy of the ministerial post, saying that that he had been vice-chairman of the Labour Party. Following the appointment of Niamh Breathnach (then chairperson) as Minister, the post became vacant and, as vice chairman, Kemmy became chairman automatically. He was not appointed by Dick Spring, and it was not a compensation for his exclusion from cabinet, reported Kemmy.[13] Ray Kavanagh explained to the author how Jim Kemmy became chairman:

Mervyn Taylor had been chair of the Labour Party and was being replaced. Niamh Breathnach defeated Emmet Stag for the Chair of the Labour Party: this was part of Spring's work to take control of the Labour Party in 1989. Jim Kemmy became vice-chair in 1991; this was a natural appointment, voted at the annual conference at the time. Kemmy was seen as a unifying force, acceptable to the full range of interests within the Labour Party. Niamh

Breathnach became minister in 1992, and Jim Kemmy automatically became chairman.

Nevertheless, Kemmy became recognised as a dissenting voice within the Labour Party. Rumours abounded about Jim Kemmy, particularly given his record in bringing down the Fine Gael-Labour coalition in 1982 on a budget vote. In the Dáil, he was observed refusing to applaud his government's budget speech, and the rumour was spreading that he would even vote against it later that evening. But the rumour was groundless. While there were aspects of the budget that Kemmy did not like, he reported to the media that Labour would be having to support a much worse budget if it was in coalition with Fine Gael and the Progressive Democrats.

According to Jan O'Sullivan:

Jim Kemmy always reserved the right to be critical of Dick Spring. He felt that Spring and his ministers had distanced themselves from the party – the perception was that Dick Spring kept himself apart. Kemmy felt that Dick Spring needed to keep both feet on the ground, so to speak.

Ray Kavanagh gave the author his own views on the controversy:

In the formation of the new collation with Fianna Fáil in 1992/3, Kemmy had made it clear he did not like coalition with Fianna Fáil. But, with the success of Labour in the elections, Spring was all-powerful. Spring might certainly have been influenced by what he saw as Kemmy's hostile attitude to Fianna Fáil. The main leaders on the 'left' were Michael D. Higgins, Emmet Stagg and Mervyn Taylor, all of them being given ministerial posts. Maybe there was niggling jealousy of Jim Kemmy – his name was being mentioned in the media as a potential minister. The whole process was very hurtful to Jim Kemmy, the

Irish Times had a list of prospective ministers, including Kemmy. Jim Kemmy was sure of an appointment to the cabinet, then it didn't happen. Everybody was ecstatic with their own appointments, but Kemmy felt deeply disappointed. That dominated his life to the end: Jim Kemmy was disillusioned, he never forgave Spring and Finlay. He felt insulted.

In the best of times, Dick Spring and Fergus Finlay would not have got on with Jim Kemmy. There was a complete lack of chemistry – they were strict and formal, Kemmy was a bundle of passion and emotion. There were different styles – Spring was very competitive, Jim Kemmy was more conciliatory.

However, quite apart from all these factors, there might have been, within the rank-and-file Labour Party, some lingering resentment on what many would have felt was Kemmy's 'betrayal' of the Labour movement by causing the collapse of the 1982 government. Some memories never die, and the persistence of such antagonisms could well have been enough to scupper Kemmy's chances of a ministerial post. A further issue could have been Kemmy's close association with the trade union movement, and his record of being on the left-wing of the party, something that might not have been attractive to the middle-class voters Labour was targeting.

But maybe Kemmy's failure to win a ministerial post was for the best. Niall Greene told the author:

Jim might not have been happy being a minister. A minister's job can be very frustrating, it not only involves having lots of vision (which Jim certainly had, he was very clear on what he wanted to achieve) and an eye for management details to make sure things were happening. His record as Chair of the Labour Party, a position requiring many of the same skills as a Minister, suggest that he would have been well up to the job but he would probably have been very frustrated at how slowly things can move in government.

This was confirmed by Joe Wallace:

As a minister it would seem to me he would have been best served by a transformative role – say like Aneurin Bevan's role as Minister of Health and Housing in the post-war UK Labour government. I suspect he might have been stifled by the day-to-day role of a mundane ministry. In this regard some would suggest that he was constrained by his role as chairman of the Labour Party during the 1990s. The issue of how he would have performed as a minister is a matter of conjecture as he was not appointed a minister – he may however have been fortunate in not being a minister.

Dick Spring told the author:

Jim Kemmy certainly became more distant after the controversy over the cabinet appointment. He tended to hold his counsel on the big policy issues of the day. He became known jokingly as one of the 'plinthstones', taking the plinth outside the Dáil to make impromptu speeches to the media, very quick to voice his dissent at any opportunity.

Kemmy continued with an independent voice on several issues. He attracted headlines for his outspoken criticism of the government policy over the 'interpretative centre' at Mullaghmore (a proposed visitor centre in the Burren, County Clare, which attracted virulent opposition from environmental groups, eventually being abandoned). He also gave a curt dismissal to the mission of the deputy leader of the Labour Party and Minister for Employment and Enterprise, Ruairi

Quinn, to Boston to try to stop the closure of the very substantial Digital company in Galway.

Talking to the media at the time, Kemmy admitted he had
'a spiky image' and could 'say uncomfortable things at times'.
He agreed that he saw his role and that of the parliamentary
party as 'keeping the government up to scratch on the Joint
Programme'. He was aware of the danger that Labour ministers could be 'sucked into an ethos of clubability' inside the
cabinet, but he reported that he not see himself as playing a
'perverse' role from outside or trying to embarrass his ministerial colleagues. Kemmy made no secret that he was disappointed that he was not chosen by Dick Spring to be a minister, or even a junior minister, after he had been named in the
media as being on the short list of candidates.[14]

However, later that year, at the Labour Party conference in
Waterford, Kemmy did support the government's proposal
for a tax amnesty as a means of raising the additional funds
the exchequer needed, not only to keep the books in order
(however laudable that may be) but to fund and sustain projects without which any talk of redistribution will be so much
'hot air'.[15] Possibly reflecting his new position as chairman of
a party now in government, Kemmy voiced support for the
government's approach, saying that he was not a 'Matt Talbot
socialist' and he did not believe in people suffering.

> If we can get money into our economy which can be used
> to alleviate distress and unemployment, that is a good
> thing. I am pragmatic in that respect, so I am support-
> ing the amnesty and I am not going to change my mind.
> It had to be accepted that people with such money did
> not pay their legal taxes originally, and the aim was to
> endeavour to get it back into this State, to make those
> concerned pay some taxes on it.[16]

Dick Spring told the author:

Jim's support for the tax amnesty was very significant. Here, with major budget constraints, we had to offer a tax amnesty to defaulters for the sake of bringing some money into the exchequer coffers. Jim understood that quandary and was gracious in supporting it.

Also at the Labour conference, Kemmy used the opportunity to promote again his strident and independent views on Northern Ireland:

The rights of Northern unionists and their attachment to their British citizenship were championed at the opening of the Labour Party conference in Waterford last night when the party chairman, Mr. Jim Kemmy, called on public representatives of all hues to step up the pace of the peace process. Mr. Kemmy told delegates that, whether people in the South liked it or not, Northern unionists valued their British citizenship and did not want to be liberated by anybody, but especially not by the IRA which spoke of freeing them from the clutches of British imperialism while murdering and maiming them.[17]

Later, Kemmy reflected this view in responding to the Hume/Adams talks, warning against the danger of the government being 'manoeuvred' by the talks into a position it could not defend.[18] Dick Spring explained to the author:

We had a strong commonality of purpose on Northern Ireland. Jim had taken a very courageous stand on Northern Ireland. He understood well the concerns of Northern Unionists; this was at a time when it would be definitely unpopular. I was very comfortable with Jim Kemmy's thinking on the North – we shared the same perspectives.

Ray Kavanagh told the author that Jim Kemmy thoroughly enjoyed being chairman:

It gave him access to the media. He chaired the annual conference, and would stop speakers in middle of their presentations and disagree with them, intervening directly, happily exceeding the scope of the chairman's role! Jim Kemmy made no apologies for doing that; it was in his direct, no-nonsense nature. However, the policy role of chair was limited. Labour was in government then, so the ministers would meet among themselves, and Jim Kemmy was not part of that insider group.

Kemmy's role as chairman of the Labour Party was also acknowledged by Dick Spring:

Being chair of the Labour Party was a recognition of his stature . . . very good chair of the party, well able to conduct the annual conference, frequently with over 1,000 delegates, it was certainly no 'garden party' and Jim was well able to control the business. We had good repartee at the conferences. Once, Jim introduced me: 'now here's the man who dropped the ball for Ireland' (reference to one of my rugby mistakes), to which I replied, 'when you can play hurling for Limerick and rugby for Munster you can talk about that'. As chair, he did a great job, commanding massive respect.

Dan Miller confirmed this by telling the author:

As chairman, Jim acted as the conscience of the Labour Party, but like even religious movements, there were fringe groups who had to be controlled or brought into the mainstream someway, Jim was very good at that.

This was echoed by Niall Greene:

Jim was an excellent chairman of the Labour Party, it was like coming home for him, it was where he should have been all the time. There were lots of competing factions (although the coalition issue had been long put to bed as an issue of division) and he brought everyone together, kept things calm. He was very good not just at the national conferences, but also in the internal 'guts' of the party, he could have been chairman for ever.

Although, maybe in Kemmy's eyes, his failure to secure a ministerial post still rankled. Manus O'Riordan told the author: 'Being the chairman of the Labour Party was probably frustrating for Jim.'

Within the Dáil, Kemmy continued to make an active contribution, such as on telecommunications, parliamentary reform and broadcasting. His comments were wide-ranging, spanning several issues of public interest.

On telecommunications, he said that with the completion of the Single Market:

> . . . it is time we ended our siege mentality . . . we are living on the periphery of Europe. We should not use this as a mealy-mouthed excuse for sitting on our hands and doing nothing; rather we should use it as a stimulus to integrate with Europe and find new markets in the world.[19]

Hence, Jim Kemmy's approach to telecommunications very much reflected his views about the urgency of European integration. On parliamentary reform, Kemmy said:

> The Dáil has been largely unreformed since it was first set up, 71 years ago. . . . We need practical reform of the Dáil and mature Dáil Members who will not make a 'Muppet Show' of Question Time and the Order of Business.[20]

This comparison of the Dáil with the 'Muppets' (a popular satirical television show at the time) was typical of Kemmy's direct style. On broadcasting, Kemmy reported: 'We need more documentaries. The local radio stations have made

very few documentaries – they have wall-to-wall music pro-
grammes and talk shows but not enough documentaries.' Reflecting his union experience, Kemmy continued: 'RTÉ has
often been bedevilled by individuals who have tried to use
the trade union movement for perverse reasons. They have
distorted the performance and image of RTÉ.'[21]

Outside the forum of the Dáil, Kemmy continued to voice
criticisms of policies in Ireland, such as calling for the option
of multi-denominational education to be made available to all
parents in the State. Speaking at the publication in Dublin of
'Intolerance in the Irish School System', a pamphlet issued by
the Campaign to Separate Church and State, Jim Kemmy said
that there should be a workable opt-out clause from religious
instruction and that there was a need for a clear definition of
the rights of minorities to be enshrined in law.[22]

Kemmy also maintained his international interests, being
one of three TDs as an Irish delegation overseeing elections in
Lesotho, at the request of the United Nations in 1993.[23]

During 1994, Kemmy, in his role as Chairman of the Labour Party, began to voice serious criticisms of the Fianna Fáil
leadership in the government. Jim Kemmy could do this as
his position of chairman, outside the government, simultaneously giving him a strong national profile without necessarily
creating instability for the coalition government. The inherent dynamics of the coalition were enough to hold it together,
Dick Spring told the author:

> Kemmy's criticisms were not de-stabilising for the coali-
> tion – the need to hold on to power superseded every-
> thing. We had experience of three elections in eighteen
> months in the 1980s, and the toll in every way was hor-
> rendous on all of us. The politicians were hungry for sta-
> bility and continuity – there was no appetite to go back to
> the electoral chaos of the early 1980s.

In early 1994, Kemmy warned the then Minister for Finance, Bertie Ahern, to 'tread warily' in any attempt to restrict mortgage interest tax relief in the coming budget.[24] Later in the same year, with the publication of the controversial Beef Tribunal report on irregularities in the beef industry during the previous Fianna Fáil administration, Kemmy said that the findings would have 'serious implications' for the two coalition parties, maintaining that the then taoiseach, Albert Reynolds, had insulted the intelligence of the public by issuing statements to the effect that he had been totally vindicated by the tribunal report, even before the findings had been published. He added: 'You cannot run a government by PR.'[25]

Also in 1994, Kemmy was nominated as Labour candidate for the European parliamentary elections, but failed to get elected by a wide margin. He attributed his party's poor performance in the European elections to a public perception that Labour was complacent in Government,[26] reflecting his uneasiness in collaboration with Fianna Fáil.

Towards the end of 1994, the crisis of the Beef Tribunal was followed by a controversy over the appointment of the Attorney General as President of the High Court, resulting in the withdrawal of Labour from government and the collapse of the Reynolds coalition:

> The taoiseach, Albert Reynolds, was likened to Rambo, a bellicose creature intent on having his way. It was one of the kinder comparisons. The Labour party chairman, Mr. Jim Kemmy, declared that Mr. Reynolds 'cannot behave like Rambo, all gung-ho one day and cooing like a dove the next'. That is not the way to run a government or behave towards partners, he said. Reading from notes well peppered with colourful analogies, he said the party had been 'taunted for too long' by the jibe of Sean Lemass, which suggested that, in a crisis, Labour wrestled with its

conscience and, unfortunately, its conscience always lost. 'This time, our conscience must win,' he said.[27]

This was followed by the formation of a new 'Rainbow Coalition' of Fine Gael, Labour and the Democratic Left, 1994–97, led by taoiseach John Bruton. Dick Spring told the author:

> Bruton turned out to be an excellent taoiseach, with all the conflicting interests around the cabinet table: Fine Gael, Democratic Left, Labour Party. But Fine Gael and Democratic Left had both been in opposition together during the previous administration, and they had forged a positive working relationship, in spite of their ideological differences. This common experience gave them a strong basis for working together.

Kemmy was an active supporter of the new coalition. Joe Kemmy told the author that Jim Kemmy had a natural antipathy to Fianna Fáil: he believed they were too long in power, were too nationalistic and excessively linked to big business. 'In contrast, he felt that Garret Fitzgerald and John Bruton were honest.' Jan O'Sullivan reported that Kemmy hated the taint of corruption that he perceived in Fianna Fáil: 'He felt they were creaming off the country, also their nationalism incensed him. He felt much more close to the 'Rainbow Coalition' with Fine Gael.'

As a result, Jim Kemmy displayed a positive approach to many proposals from the new government. For example, on the Abortion Information Bill in 1995, he said Labour would be supporting the bill, which was agreed by the government, and would not break ranks, even though the bill did not go far enough:

> It is an altered bill and doesn't meet with Labour criteria but we are in Government with two other parties now. The bill reflects the reality of the attitudes in the Dáil.

Members do have misgivings but we will be supporting it
if it is challenged.[28]

In 1996, he supported the government budget, even through
SIPTU (Services, Industrial, Professional and Technical Union
– Ireland's largest trade union with 200,000 members) had
criticised it:

> The budget encourages industrial development and job
> creation. For too long Members of this House, represen-
> tatives of the trade union movement, the Church and oth-
> er bodies paid lip service to the long-term unemployed
> and lower-paid workers. No positive acti.. ...as taken to
> tackle those problems. . . . I too read SIPTU's reported
> critical comments on the budget. . . . I am still involved
> in the trade union movement and I take what the move-
> ment says seriously. SIPTU was especially critical of the
> government policy to give £80 per week to employers who
> take on a long-term unemployed person for three years
> or more. I analysed their criticisms but the reality is that
> the government had to discriminate in favour of the long-
> term unemployed.[29]

In the same speech, Kemmy demonstrated what he called
his 'people-centred' approach. This was in a call for positive
policy in tackling crime, arguing that there were no simple or
easy answers and all sections of society must contribute to the
solution of the problem. The government must give leadership in tackling crime and the government has taken the first
step to tackle it, said Kemmy.

> We must try as best we can to create a genuine infrastruc-
> ture whereby people can lead decent lives. That is what
> party politics is about. Ideology should serve people, not
> the other way round. For too long in all parties we bowed
> to ideology but that is the wrong attitude. We have to be

flexible to solve problems and build a society in which people can live decent and crime free lives.

This people-centred approach was also reflected in a later contribution on another topic: 'Ideology, whether it be in respect of Sinn Féin, nationalism or socialism, must serve people, not the other way around.'

Was Jim Kemmy frustrated by lack of power? 'I don't think so,' Dick Spring said to the author:

> Jim was focused on Limerick and the need to improve conditions for people there. He carried the *Angela's Ashes* burden on how working people were treated, told to wait and queue for everything while the middle and upper classes got the favours. Jim Kemmy was a real believer in equality for people, so that would have been his focus, not power.

In April 1997, the Labour Party conference was held in Limerick. Looking to the forthcoming election, Jim Kemmy called on delegates to remember the vision of the Labour Party, especially its fight against poverty and lack of opportunity. According to Kavanagh, it was a speech of 'great sincerity and passion, a very fitting swan song for Labour's gentle giant'. Reflecting on the TD's life, Ray Kavanagh told the author:

> Kemmy broadened the horizons of the Labour Party, broadened the scope, instilled respect for Labour, Kemmy was an idealist, he enhanced politics. Kemmy had a status about him that has not been replaced, he was big moderniser in the trade union movement. Jim Kemmy reached out to people.

Joe Wallace reported:

> Jim was ahead of the curve on social developments such as contraception and family planning. He identified clearly

the conservatism and reactionary aspects of Ireland of the 1960s to 1980s and named these publicly, which took courage and resolve. In taking strong and controversial stances he was both electorally punished, as in the abortion issue, and rewarded, as in his stance on provisional Sinn Féin and the North. Despite loosing his Dáil seat in 1982, in the long run he was rewarded for these stances. By the time of his death he was acknowledged nationally as being principled and fearless in the stances he took.

The following election in June 1997 proved a disaster for Labour, with a collapse by half from 33 seats to just 17. Jim Kemmy retained his seat, although with a substantially reduced vote, reflecting this national decline of Labour.

Endnotes

1. *Irish Times*, 27 February 1993

2. Dáil debates, 23 April 1987.

3. Dáil debates, 3 December 1987.

4. Dáil debates, 1 December 1988.

5. Dáil debates, 9 Feb 1989.

6. Dáil debates 25 May 1989.

7. Dáil debates, 3 July 1989.

8. Dáil debates, 12 July 1989.

9. Correspondence between Dick Spring and Jim Kemmy, January 1993 (Kemmy Collection, UL).

10. *Snakes and Ladders* by Fergus Finlay (New Island, Dublin, 1998).

11. *Limerick Leader*, 16 January 1993.

12. *Spring and the Labour Party* by Stephen Collins (The O'Brien Press, Dublin, 1993).

13. *Limerick Leader*, 1 January 1994.

14. *Irish Times*, 27 February 1993.

15. *Irish Times*, 5 April 1993.

16. *Irish Times*, 3 June 1993.

17. *Irish Times*, 3 April 1993.

18. *Irish Times*, 28 October 1993.

19. Dáil debates, 28 May 1992.

20. Dáil debates, 1993.

21. Dáil debates, 6 May 1993.

22. *Irish Times*, 1 Oct 1993.

23. *Limerick Leader*, 29 March 1993.

24. *Irish Times*, 18 January 1994.

25. *Irish Times*, 4 August 1994.

26. *Irish Times*, 14 June 1994.

27. *Irish Times*, 14 November 1994.

28. *Irish Times*, 23 February 1995.

29. Dáil debates, 1 February 1996.

5

Local Government

While Jim Kemmy's political life at national level was developing and enlarging over the 1970s, 1980s and 1990s, he was active at the local level as well. His work in Limerick similarly demonstrated the factors influencing Kemmy's approach, expressing themselves in two ways: Kemmy as local representative and Kemmy as writer. Patsy Harrold, Jim Kemmy's friend, told the author: 'Jim's local politics was initially all about socialism, but it later enlarged to other themes like heritage and history, his background as a stonemason was a huge influence.'

Jim Kemmy's local political activities focused on his role as a councillor in Limerick City Council, being initially elected in 1974, one of only two independents at the time on the Council. Prior to then, regulations prevented employees of local authorities from simultaneously acting as public representatives, thus Kemmy's role as stonemason in Limerick City Council barred him from such participation. However, removal of this restriction created the opportunity for Kemmy to go for election, securing almost 1,300 votes in his ward, out of a poll of 6,800.[1] This was a substantial achievement for someone outside the mainstream political parties. According to the *Limerick Leader*:

> The election has raised many talking points. Councillor Kemmy's rise to public life is a major surprise to many people. Certainly most expected the Garryowen man to poll well but even his most loyal supporters would not have anticipated such a massive first preference vote.[2]

At his first meeting of the Council, Kemmy established his credentials as a sharp critic, calling for a meeting for an emergency housing programme for St. Mary's Park. He also hit out at the use of Council members' robes, and re-iterated his pre-election pledge that he would not wear a robe, arguing that the distinctive dress only distanced the elected representatives from the democratic process.

Kemmy felt excluded from official organisations, objecting to the way party machines were electing people to bodies. He believed he had more right to be on those bodies because of his high poll, arguing that the people he was elected to represent were being denied representation so that party men could take the various positions to be filled. 'People who just scrape into Council get these positions.'[3] Joe Kemmy told the author:

> A lot of the other councillors refused to acknowledge Jim's existence, he was treated like a pariah, they looked on him as an extreme socialist or a communist, this made him bitter. The other councillors kept him out of every committee possible, he was excluded from many key representations, such as the mayoralty.

However Kemmy was made chairman of the Council's National Monuments Committee, an advisory group on the care of national monuments in the city. This was not a position in which other councillors had much interest, and was thus open to Kemmy – and it was to play a very significant role in his later development.

Kemmy used his role in the Council to take strong stands on several controversial issues. He boycotted a civic reception to welcome the new Catholic Bishop Jeremiah Newman: 'The opinion of a Bishop should be of no more value than the opinion of an informed lay person. It is about time this fact was understood in Ireland.' Although Pat Reeves told the author: 'When Jim refused to attended the consecration of the new Bishop he was heavily criticised by some neighbours in Garryowen who supported the Bishop. "You should be there representing us," they told him angrily!

In the same speech, Kemmy argued that the Government and councils are merely the executive committee of the employers and wealthy elements of society: 'Their main function is to keep the system going to ensure that the wealth of the society stays in a minority of hands.' Kemmy reported he had received over 600 complaints since his election but there was little the structure of local government could do about all these issues.[4]

Kemmy's local political activities took more and more of his time. As a result, he resigned from his position as chairman of Limerick Trades Council to concentrate on being a councillor.[5] He continued to persistently criticise local government systems, arguing that 'the real everyday power of working decisions does not rest with councillors. The city manager and his officials are frequently not influenced by council debates when making decisions.' Although, on the council officials, he said that he got on well with them but that a few had been unhelpful.[6]

Kemmy was an active commentator on development projects in the city, for example, arguing that plans for the brick in the new City Hall should harmonise with the Georgian nature of the city.

'He was sorry that there were no stone features' in the proposed structure. Also, work by local artists should be purchased and put on display. Kemmy supported a plan to draw up a full scheme for the restoration of King John's Castle. He criticised the opening of a housing pilot scheme in St Mary's Park as 'ballyhoo with screaming headlines and photographs. Beyond this, nothing much had been done in housing. We should not sit down and clap ourselves on the back.' Kemmy also called for acceleration of the housing programme in Moyross.[7]

He continued his conflict with the Church authorities. Kemmy participated in a deputation from a public meeting to meet Bishop Newman about the appointment of a clerk in one particular parish. The mood at the meeting had been in favour of the incumbent temporary clerk: 'People at the top cannot dictate to people at the bottom – people are entitled to have a say in who their parish clerk should be – people are entitled to get full information, the days of the closed shop are gone.'[8]

Bishop Newman accused politicians of being silent on the Shannon Airport stopover controversy, 'they summon up crocodile tears', implicating Kemmy. Jim Kemmy replied that the Bishop had been noted for his own silence on other important issues, but that politicians had been restrained in not criticising Newman for this. 'We let him off the hook,' retorted Kemmy. 'I am a democrat, Bishop Newman does not understand democracy.' To which Newman replied, 'I have lectured in political theory and I do not share his irrelevant references to it.'[9] Ray Kavanagh told the author that he believed that Bishop Newman was afraid of Jim Kemmy's moral authority, and felt threatened by it.

Persons who criticise the absence of halting sites without even offering alternatives were themselves criticised by Jim Kemmy, referring to religious orders in particular. This followed criticisms from a congregation of religious sisters in

Limerick about the city's failure to provide halting sites. 'Nuns have never nominated a halting site, that would be a positive development,' argued Kemmy.[10]

In 1979, Kemmy condemned the 'underhand' manner in which the Pope and three other clergy – Cardinal Tomás O Fiaich, Dr Alibrandi (papal nuncio) and Bishop Newman – were conferred with the freedom of the city. 'The whole thing has become a farce,' said Kemmy. Only the Pope should be made a freeman. 'The freedom of the city should only be conferred after clear thought and serious deliberation. The decision to confer the four was rushed through,' said Kemmy. An attempt was made by Kemmy and others to reverse the Council's decision to grant freedom of the city to the full four clergy. 'The majority party could now make the freedom to anybody they liked – this made a political football out of the whole thing,' said Jim Kemmy.[11]

A refusal by Bishop Jerimiah Newman to allow the city's mayor, Councillor Jan O'Sullivan, who was a member of the Church of Ireland, to read a lesson at a Mass to launch Limerick Civic Week in 1994 was opposed by Kemmy. This was reported not to be in line with the Catholic Church's revised Directory of Ecumenism, which allows readings by members of other churches 'on exceptional occasions'. At the time, Kemmy called on Dr. Newman to apologise for the way in which the mayor had been treated.[12]

Kemmy regularly challenged Bishop Jeremiah Newman on many issues, the two being sharply divided by the Bishop's ardent Catholicism versus Kemmy's robust atheism. But this divide, although deep, was not wide and was easily bridged by the two men's shared passion for local history and local community, with long phone conversations between the two into the night on all the current topics on culture and heritage. At the time, rumours were rife about the Bishop's heavy drink-

ing, although a Church spokesman denied that Bishop Newman was receiving treatment for alcoholism.[13] Kemmy (not a
significant drinker) participated actively in these late-night
chats with Newman. The Bishop also contributed articles to
Kemmy's local history periodical *Old Limerick Journal*. 'It was
a funny sort of relationship, they had respect for each other,
enjoyed robust conversations together, although dogmatically
different on religious issues,' said Jan O'Sullivan. 'In spite of
everything, the two got on like a house on fire,' reported Patsy
Harrold.

This colourful relationship between Kemmy the politician
and Newman the Bishop was confirmed to the author by Dan
Miller:

> One of the unique qualities of Jim was that he never per-
> sonalised anything in his arguments, kept things at the
> political level. When Jeremiah Newman first came to
> Limerick, Jim wrote against the idea of a reception for
> the new Bishop, the reception being against the vow of
> poverty. Later Jeremiah effectively lost Jim the seat over
> the abortion controversy, but Jim never got bitter about
> that. Our offices were close together in the Mechanics'
> Institute, and Jim would often get phone calls from Jer-
> emiah Newman, they would have long conversations
> about history and heritage – Jim enjoyed this discourse
> with somebody of different views to himself. There was
> no bitterness about Jim, he embraced Newman in later
> life. Jim was not vindictive. In the conflict with Jeremiah
> Newman, there were rumours about an alcohol affliction
> suffered by the Bishop, with talk on the street about the
> Bishop making public appearances under the influence
> of alcohol, but Jim never exploited that rumour.

Dan Miller concluded to the author: 'Jim was definitely not
religious, but he had a lot of religious friends, he got on very
well with some of the more radical priests, those who might

have shared his left-wing views'. Seamus Harrold reported: 'Jim and the Bishop were both very alike, they were both bachelors, both passionate about their interests, both single-minded, focused on heritage issues.'

The City Council itself regularly drew his fire: 'The Council is stagnant and there is a need to jolt the manager and his officials from time to time.' According to Kemmy, the public were not aware of the difficulties faced by councillors attempting to redress grievances. The system is such that councillors all too often are used as buffers between the people and the public officials. Kemmy complained:

> The system trundles on and it does not take account of people's wishes or the representatives on the council. All too often council meetings are merely tired old rituals and excuses for a parade of hackneyed party politics and personal glorification. Invariably, council debates do not reflect the live important issues of the day.[14]

He also proposed to the Trades Council to ask the City Council to have meetings at 7.30 pm, changing from the then arrangement of 4.30 pm meetings. Kemmy's argument was that this would better facilitate public attendance, although this was opposed by the Local Government and Public Service Union who did not want their members to be forced to attend late meetings.[15]

The role of mayor was an issue that attracted his attention. At one stage, Kemmy put himself forward for mayor, aiming to demonstrate that there was no real political difference between the main parties. 'I am pleased that my candidature has flushed the coalition of convenience into full public view.' Fianna Fáil and Fine Gael had carved out the mayoralty between them for the duration of the City Council.

It is extremely unfair that four members of the City Council should hold the mayoral office for two terms while
other members have not been afforded the opportunity of
serving even one period. It is most degrading and undemocratic that the highest office in the city should be passed
around as a political plaything in this cynical manner.

Kemmy called for an end to the 'abuse' and said the election
of mayor should be entrusted to the people in the local elections.[16]

Kemmy's attitude to local developments was influenced by
his wider perspectives. Calling for the acceleration of housing developments, he claimed that land in Ireland has always
been canonised in the past and private property was well protected by the three main political parties. Money appeared to
be flowing in the private housing area and some of this should
be channelled into the public house building sector.[17] Kemmy
protested against the destruction of the home of Brian Mer-
riman, the eighteenth century poet, by the City Council. The
house was demolished to make way for a roundabout and
Kemmy described the action as insensitive and carried out in
a brutal way, although the city architect responded that the
building had no architectural or archaeological significance,
and that a memorial plaque would be erected.[18]

Seamus Harrold gave some other examples:

Jim would lobby for preservation of all sorts of things,
like the chapel in Cratloe a beautiful nineteenth century
barn church, really unique, that the parish priest wanted
to demolish. Jim lobbied the bishop and succeeded in its
preservation. Later, at the time of the development of
the Hunt Museum, the City Council wanted to do it in
red brick, but Jim was horrified at that; he wanted it in
stone and successfully lobbied to ensure the stone was
retained.

Social conditions in the city were highlighted. He talked about 'anarchy' in Ballinacurra Weston. The army should be called in to quell the state of anarchy in the vicinity of the Hyde Road shops where vandalism has resulted in substantial damage. Shops have been torn asunder and firemen trying to fight fires faced a fusillade of stones. Vandals have caused substantial damage to council houses over 18 months, more than the entire housing maintenance budget, reported Kemmy.[19] In a University of Limerick summer school, he recalled commentators in 1912 struck by 'huddled people in their houses' in Limerick. Kemmy compared this to the building of the city's large housing estates on the north and south side of Limerick. 'Have we learned anything since those days? We still huddle the people in large housing estates.'[20] Kemmy's involvement in social groups in the city included his assistance to the Boherbuoy Brass band in securing a new hall in 1976, a contribution that won him the post of honorary vice-chairman of the band.

The issue of water charges was one that continually beset the City Council. Ireland has been unusual in Europe in not charging domestic consumers directly for use of water, with any proposals to introduce such charges always generating intense opposition. In 1985, the estimates meeting of the Council was adjourned in an uproar, disrupted by protestors objecting to the imposition of water charges – the 'Coordinating Committee against Water Tax'. Kemmy said that the group might be vociferous, but they had a genuine grievance. All opposed water rates, he said, and they intended to discuss the issue. On another occasion, the threat of dissolution hung over Limerick City Council following their failure to strike a rate (local property tax, levied on commercial premises) at an estimates meeting. Jim Kemmy argued that he was in no doubt that rates should be opposed entirely. It was a case that they could not make ends meet simply because they had not been given enough money from central government to run the city. 'I have every sympathy for the city manager but we have imposed rates on people who oppose them – the burden seems to be falling on the PAYE sector all the time.'[21]

Kemmy exploited his council role to make inputs on international issues. In 1979, citing himself as the leader of the anti-apartheid movement in Limerick, Kemmy promised that there would be a sizeable demonstration if the South African rugby team came to Limerick on a visit proposed at the time. He was roundly criticised by other councillors for this – the team was actually the South African 'Barbarians', a mixed-race team unlike the all-white 'Springboeks'.[22] Later, in 1990, he launched a scathing attack on the Department of Justice for the evasive manner in which they were treating the case of a Somali refugee then in his seventh week in the Limerick prison without trial, having jumped an Aeroflot flight at Shannon. Jim Kemmy compared this case to the situation of thousands of Irish people working illegally in the US: 'We expect them to be treated well and to be given green cards and any entitlements they require. We cannot point the finger at the US when we see the manner we are treating this refugee,' said Kemmy.[23]

Criticisms of Kemmy were many, and came from several quarters.

In the 1970s, Kemmy's Limerick Family Planning group were accused of comprising one political clique – 'that of Councillor Jim Kemmy and his supporters'. They were criticised for failing to establish a full medical clinic. The attack came from Ernest Fitzgerald of the Southill Association. According to Fitzgerald, the proposed constitution of the clinic would ensure that 'Kemmy and his supporters will dominate the committee in future. Committee members will nominate new members.' The clinic is often described as the 'Kemmy clinic' and under these circumstances it will not attract more members, argued Ernest Fitzgerald.[24] But there may have been political undercurrents here. According to Joe Kemmy, Ernest Fitzgerald was a Sinn Féin activist: 'Jim was happy to get out of the Family Planning Clinic once it got established.'

Kemmy's attacks on the Catholic Church was disputed by community activist Noel Hannon, accusing Kemmy of ignoring the work of the religious orders in caring for the less well-off members of society. Hannon had organised a group lobbying for resources for a brain-damaged girl, and accused Kemmy of not attending any of their public meetings, even though he had been invited to come.[25]

A potential opponent was Willie O Dea, the Fianna Fáil TD for East Limerick, arguing that Kemmy consistently used the poor people of Limerick for political advantage:

> Deputy Kemmy would get a heart attack if poverty were to disappear because he is one of the politicians who feed on poverty and the difficulties of the poor people, he is like a vulture, but doing nothing about it, he has a vested interest in seeing poverty continue.[26]

Although, according to Niall Greene, these onslaughts were purely at the political level, and did not descend to personal enmity, recounting this incident to the author:

> One example of the networking of local politics was on the last occasion on which I had a pint with Jim before his final illness, Willie O'Dea came in with some of his followers, went over to another corner engaged in busy conversation, but in a matter of moments, Willie was over to Jim, both engaging in active conversation on the latest political happenings, who was doing what, what was going on, the current issues.

Despite the many controversies of his life, or maybe because of them, Kemmy secured significant local support, winning the position of alderman (senior councillor with a large number of votes) in 1979. Seamus Harrold commented:

> In the 1979 elections he topped the poll, becoming senior alderman. This was a big transformation reflecting a lot of work on the ground – he did a lot of work on unfair dismissals, many people came to him to be represented at these hearings and it won him a lot of goodwill.

The next year, in 1980, Kemmy became chairman of the Arts Committee of the City Council, reflecting his active interest in that area. His contribution was to substantially raise the profile of the arts, particularly strengthening the position of the art gallery, and promoting the Exhibition of Visual Arts (EVA). In later years, after his death, this contribution by Jim Kemmy was acknowledged by a special exhibition and publication of Limerick art, showing how contemporary artists could develop their work, stimulated by work from previous centuries.[27]

Kemmy's policies towards Northern Ireland were not restricted to the national scene, generating local controversies in 1981 through his opposition to the H-block hunger strike. This was a protest by republican prisoners seeking special category status, resulting in the deaths of ten prisoners and radicalising public opinion in Ireland. Kemmy's argument that the Northern unionist majority deserved recognition, combined with his opposition to the hunger strike, attracted virulent criticisms from several local groups in Limerick. Seamus Harrold said: 'We took on the H-block republican vote, we did not care, Jim's anti-nationalist policies made complete sense. He had contact with several Unionist political leaders, and would receive correspondence and cards from them.'

Kemmy's work as a councillor was rewarded by his election as mayor on two occasions, 1991 and 1995, made possible by a new majority coalition on the City Council, comprising Labour, Progressive Democrats, Workers Party and independents.

In 1991, following his election, Kemmy said:

I am the first building worker, the first building crafts-man and the first mason ever to be elected mayor. I am the first socialist of my kind to be elected in this office. It might be considered strange that workers who built this city would have to wait for so long to see one of their col-leagues elected to mayor of Limerick but such is the case . . . I have come to this office with only one objective: to serve Limerick and its people to the very best of my abil-ity. I have no recrimination with others who have been somewhat less than flattering about me. This is a day for celebration, not recrimination. Tonight, the slate is wiped clean as far as I am concerned, for everybody with whom I have crossed swords, inside and outside this chamber. At all times, we must manage our city in the interests of our citizens and not of our ideology. Ideology must serve people and not the other way around and it must never be allowed to become our political slave-master.[28]

He said that key issues facing Limerick were its image, housing renewal and the need for decentralisation, and con-cluded: 'Let us get on with the business of running our city well and in improving its appearance and our image will soon take care of itself.'

Margaret O'Donoghue noted:

Jim knew from past experience that the night of the may-oral election could see any upset, and he could never be sure of being elected. He had prepared his 25-page speech but warned me, 'don't give it out to the press until you see the chain going on my neck' – he could never be certain until the vote.

Kemmy gave his mayoralty some distinctive flavours. One of his early official receptions was for a local darts team, height-ening their profile. He had active involvements with the Pike

Rovers Football Club and the Boherbuoy Brass Band. But one other group he specifically touched was the British Legion, Kemmy being the first Limerick mayor to officially attend the Remembrance Day commemoration of Limerick men killed in the First World War. At a later event, Kemmy was reported to have impressed a group of visiting British journalists with his strong grasp of the links between several prominent British writers and Limerick.

'As mayor, he worked more from the trade union offices in the Mechanics' Institute rather than City Hall, felt more at home there,' said Margaret O'Donoghue.

> But one change was that being made mayor forced Jim Kemmy to buy a new suit and get his hair cut. He was always spending his money on books, clothes were totally secondary – one day after a heavy cloudburst he had to take off his rain-sodden shoe in the office with a large hole in it!

Patsy Harrold echoed this: 'Being made mayor was the one chance I got to get Jim to buy a new suit – he hated spending money on clothes.'

But controversy was never far away. Completing his first term as mayor, and handing over to the new mayor, a Progressive Democrat, Jim Kemmy cautioned his replacement that a vote of no confidence would be declared if he tried to use the mayoralty to political advantage of the Progressive Democrats. This was rejected by the Progressive Democrats as it was inevitable that a mayor would reflect the views of his own party, as indeed Jim Kemmy had done himself, they retorted.[29]

Both as mayor of Limerick, and at other times in the 1990s, Kemmy exploited his national and local positions to focus attention of several challenges of importance to him.

Entry to secondary schools was a controversial issue in the city. Changes in the system of entry to second level schools in

Limerick had caused widespread public controversy and concerns, particularly among parents, reported Kemmy in 1991.[30]

The system was imposed by the principals and vice-principals association, acting as a cartel, where there was no appeal procedure, no accountability, and by a process whereby, for the most part, secret selection criteria were applied, complained Jim Kemmy.

In 1993, Kemmy lobbied the then Minister for Education, Niamh Breathnach, on the issue. The Minister reported that her department's primary objective was to ensure that all the schools in a catchment area had provision to meet demand for places. Intake policy was essentially a matter for each post-primary school management, subject to the application of acceptable criteria. However, the Minister agreed that difficulties had arisen in relation to admissions to post-primary schools in Limerick, and about problems experienced by a number of pupils attaining second-level places in the Limerick area. As a result, the Christian Brothers set up a junior second level school for boys at St. Munchins National School to resolve the problem on the north side of the city. Agreement was also reached with a number of schools in the south side of the city to provide extra places for local pupils who had still not been placed in a second level school.

Art and artists attracted his increasing attention. In September 1994, Jim Kemmy helped with the organisation of a local display of the UTV (Ulster Television) collection – 150 works of art, probably the largest collection of its kind in Northern Ireland. The display was opened by the then Tánaiste, Dick Spring.[31]

'On a local level, Jim Kemmy put a lot of pressure on Ministers to secure projects for Limerick – City Art Gallery, Hunt Museum, main drainage, schools investments in Limerick,' said Jan O'Sullivan.

At an opening of an exhibition of painting by Limerick artist John Shinnors at the Belltable Arts Centre in 1984,[32] Kemmy gave a robust justification of a socialist's approach to art:

> We do not usually associate the name of Lenin with art, but he once said 'art belongs to the people. Its roots should penetrate deeply into the very thick of the masses of the people. It should be comprehensible to these masses and loved by them. It should unite the emotions, the thoughts and the will of these masses and raise them to a higher level.' In Ireland, our neglect of the visual arts has been notorious. Government have made a poor response. In the absence of this kind of response from public bodies, people can help the artists by buying their work. Instead of giving the more conventional types of presents to our relatives at Christmas and birthdays, we could give paintings.
>
> Unlike science, which reduces reality to a blue print or formula, the images of art reveal reality in its infinite diversity and many-sided richness.

Kemmy concluded this speech by condemning 'the havoc which a half-century of philistinism and unbridled gombeen commercialism have wrought with the aesthetic sensibility of our people.'

'Every Friday night during the 1990s, he would leave his clinic and across go to the Art Gallery in case anything was on,' said Jan O'Sullivan.

In July 1992, a 'Church and State Walk' by Jim Kemmy as mayor and Bishop Edward Darling (Church of Ireland) from Cork to Limerick to raise funds for local charities, with farewell ceremony by the Mayor of Cork and local politicians, secured £8,000. 'That was a big effort,' reported Margaret O'Donoghue, 'the walk took a full week, and Jim had blisters for days afterwards, he could only wear slippers, but it was good teamwork, the religious bishop and the ardent socialist!'

In 1993, Jim Kemmy lobbied Minister for Arts and Culture, Michael D. Higgins, for support for the new Hunt Museum, subsequently opening in 1996, with assistance for capital investment through the European Structural Funds

On his election in 1995 as mayor for the second time, Jim Kemmy said, 'cities are not museum pieces and it is essential for Limerick to retain the best of its cultural and physical heritage while at the same time, ensuring it is not left behind in a rapidly changing world'. Key issues highlighted by Kemmy in that speech included enlightened urban renewal through a good mix of public and private enterprise, construction of smaller housing estates in the inner city, proper funding for local authorities, the need for a city boundary extension, the new Hunt Museum, the forthcoming 800th anniversary of the city, unemployment, Northern Ireland and sport.[33] Kemmy's second term as mayor was un-scheduled, and was brought about by the sudden withdrawal (for personal reasons) of the previously agreed Labour candidate.

As mayor, Kemmy pleaded for unity of purpose between city and county, highlighting the example of the combined city and county support for Cork as one for Limerick interests to follow.[34] Ray Kavanagh said:

> Jim Kemmy was very good for Limerick, he was a very presentable person. Kemmy could defend Limerick vigorously; the negative reputation of Limerick developed after his death – he would have been a great defender of Limerick had he lived longer.

The link between Jim Kemmy and the Kemmy Business School in the University of Limerick was established at this time. J.P. McManus, a Limerick-born businessman and financier, and funding sponsor of the Business School, had accumulated substantial wealth through bookmaking and currency exchange. McManus had a connection with Kemmy through their shared experience as past pupils of the Christian Brothers school in Sexton Street. The two enjoyed a friendship and, during a visit to McManus's house in Martinstown, County Limerick, Kemmy, struck by the scale of the house, enquired where the library was, to which McManus had to admit, 'we don't have any, only racing magazines!' Within a matter of days, McManus received from Kemmy a gift of several books, from Kemmy's own personal collection, as a start-up contribution to his library. Years afterwards, Joe Kemmy enquired from McManus on his motivation in sponsoring the Kemmy Business School at the University of Limerick, and in suggesting that the school be named after Kemmy: 'Do you not remember the incident about the books?' replied McManus.

Later that year, in his mayoral capacity, Kemmy was honoured by a special presentation from Israel, becoming one of the first public representatives to be presented with the new 'Medal of the City of Jerusalem'. Mr. Zvi Gabay, the Israeli ambassador to Ireland, said he admired Mr Kemmy's work as a public representative. The two had met at the Labour Party annual conference in the University of Limerick. 'I was not to know at that time that he would he honoured by being elected mayor of Limerick for the second time,' he said. On that occasion, Mr. Kemmy had given him the background to the history of the Jews in Limerick and said how he had sought to have the old Jewish cemetery at Kilmurry outside Limerick restored by the Council. The work was later taken up by the Limerick Civic Trust.[35]

Jim Kemmy was also honoured in the same year by Professor John A. Murphy of University College Cork. At a function in 1995 to celebrate the publication of a history of UCC by the professor, it was reported:

"And I'll blow your government down"

Kemmy's controversial political life, and his frequent clashes with the governments of his day, attracted the attention of the media. (Kemmy Collection)

With actor Richard Harris (1991) (*Limerick Leader*)

In the building sites in Limerick, Jim Kemmy is young with glasses, third from left, second row (1950s) (Building and Allied Trades Union)

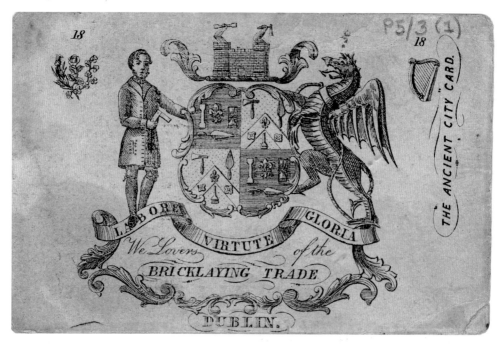

Kemmy's membership card of the bricklayers union. The detailed and intricate designs are evidence of a group who proudly saw themselves as real professionals. (1970s) (Kemmy Collection, UL)

JIM KEMMY
Uncompromised & Unafraid

┌─ A TIME FOR CHANGE ─┐
Vote No. 1 for Jim Kemmy
The Genuine Alternative

Working as a stonemason for Limerick City
Council (1960s) (*Limerick Leader*)

First election leaflet, 1977
(Kemmy Collection, UL)

Campaigning in Southill, 1977 general election (Limerick City Council)

Limerick Socialist
Kemmy Collection, UL

The life of a trade union leader inevitably meant active involvement in the day-to-day work of members *(Limerick Leader)*

Winning the election (1981). Joe Kemmy, Jim's brother, is on the right *(Limerick Leader)*

Working as a stonemason for Limerick City
Council (1960s) (*Limerick Leader*)

JIM KEMMY
Uncompromised & Unafraid

┌─ A TIME FOR CHANGE ─┐
Vote No. 1 for Jim Kemmy
The Genuine Alternative
└─────────────────────┘

First election leaflet, 1977
(Kemmy Collection, UL)

Campaigning in Southill, 1977 general election (Limerick City Council)

Kemmy combined his local commitments with an active political life at national level, seen here with Barry Desmond, TD (*Limerick Leader*)

Painting of Jim Kemmy by J. Lyons (*Limerick Leader*)

Mayor Jim Kemmy in the 1990s

Limerick Socialist
Kemmy Collection, UL

The life of a trade union leader inevitably meant active involvement in the day-to-day work of members *(Limerick Leader)*

Winning the election (1981). Joe Kemmy, Jim's brother, is on the right *(Limerick Leader)*

Old Limerick Journal
(Kemmy Collection, UL)

Arriving at Limerick City Hall
following election as TD (1981)
(Limerick Leader)

Establishment of the Democratic Socialist Party (1982) *(Irish Independent)*

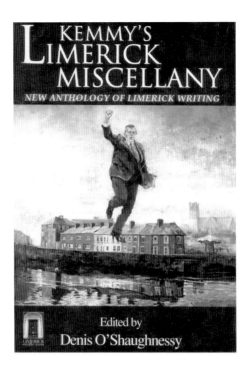

Published in 2009, *Kemmy's Limerick Miscellany* is a good illustration of Kemmy's continuing influence (Limerick Writers Centre)

Grave of Jim Kemmy (Irish Graves)

Thanking the mayor, Professor Murphy recalled Jim Kemmy's uphill struggle in attaining his present influential position in municipal and national politics. Referring to his new book, Professor Murphy said that in 1845 Limerick had lost out to Cork in the lobbying contest to secure one of the new Queen's Colleges, and had to wait a long time to secure its own place in the educational area. It was of interest that the then mayor of Limerick turned up in the Cork college for a celebratory banquet in 1850, though the other Munster public representatives deemed it more prudent to dissociate themselves from an institution regarded as 'godless' by the ecclesiastical authorities. In our own day, Mayor Kemmy had similarly courageously stood up to powerful clericalist interests.[36]

Kemmy continued to use his mayoral position to highlight many issues, such as at the launching of Help Foundation Trust, a grouping of local organisations, claiming at that event that there were 'too many charities and not enough justice in the country'.[37] 'He didn't like people to be too abstract; if he saw people doing what he saw to be progressive things, he would give a lot of support,' said Jan O'Sullivan.

In his position as local TD, Kemmy lobbied intensively for constituents[38] on a range of issues, probably reflecting the typical representation work of TDs of his time, but also displaying a passion and flair for the underdog, and a willingness to help out in all sorts of unusual controversies – support for job seekers, employment appeals, places for children in special schools. He supported specific minorities, such as the 'Limerick Tip Head Pickers' (a group of men retrieving reusable material from the city rubbish dump), as well as casual workers like part-time dockers at Limerick port. Typically, he seemed to target his support for people who, for one reason or another, did not fit the complexities of the social welfare system, frequently pleading for a sympathetic approach to applicants for assistance on the grounds of their special or unusual circumstances. One example of the length to which he would go was to write to shop-keepers and commercial traders on behalf of complaining customers, challenging the shops on issues of consumer rights around over-charging, shoddy goods, return of deposits, ill-fitting clothes, poor repair work, bad workmanship, inadequate life insurance and defective products.

While much of Kemmy's support was concentrated in the public housing schemes in the city, he drew significant votes from other areas as well. Seamus Harrold reported:

> Moyross and Southill, you could never depend on them, lucky to get one-third. Jim was picking up votes all over the place, there was no logic on how people would vote. Jim might even get second and third preferences from people voting Sinn Féin or Fianna Fáil. He was picking up friendships all over the place, people would talk to him and engage with him who would never be seen dead with him. He built up a solid reputation. He did not approve of the 'Gregory deal', where, in 1982, independent TD Tony Gregory supported the Haughey government in return for special favours for his constituency.

This was echoed by Joe Wallace:

> I found that in the 1980s he got a very warm welcome in Moyross where there were a lot of young working class people there. He was also popular in Southill where there was an older population, although Fianna Fáil also drew substantial votes there – notably Willie O'Dea. He was also well received in many middle class areas, where I suspect he would have picked up a lot of second preferences. In my experience generally it was very easy canvassing for him precisely because he was seen as principled.

But there were other sides to Kemmy, too, and yet another controversy. In his final year as mayor Jim Kemmy was reported to insist on the Garryowen Residents' Association apologising for remarks which he claimed 'abused and insulted his office'. The Residents' Association had accused Kemmy of being a 'dictator' and misrepresenting their views about a local housing controversy. Kemmy replied that 'it was unacceptable that they should be allowed abuse the First Citizen of the city in that way'.[39] Perhaps this remark encapsulates so well the 'mainstreaming' of Jim Kemmy over the years, coming a long distance from the angry rebellion of the early period and giving way to a gradual embracing of the civic institutions of his time. This was an evolution of his views that was acknowledged and accepted by Kemmy himself, perhaps growing naturally with age and time. But maybe it was 'mainstreaming' too far? Certainly the 'Younger Kemmy' would not have approved, although Joe Kemmy told the author that there were political undercurrents in this particular incident, with local Fianna Fáil activists leading the opposition to a City Council housing proposal.

Commenting on Kemmy, Anna-Maria Hajba told the author:

> In the Kemmy archives, we found a lot of ESB or TV licence bills of other people, paid by Jim Kemmy. Kemmy gave away his mayoral salary. We saw numerous letters from people facing financial hardship – he would often give them money for support. Kemmy was a socialist to the core of his being. Politically very outspoken, he worked against what he saw to be the taboos of his time. His job was his life, ate and drank socialism, his activities were all politics and trade unions.

Ray Kavanagh confirmed this, telling the author: 'Jim Kemmy gave away his money; he had nothing when he died, only the house which he left to a family member.'

Dan Miller agreed:

> Jim probably was one of the gentlest of human beings, material things were not his forte, putting beer mats into his shoes to keep out the rain from seeping through the holes in the soles of his shoes. People would come into our office at the Mechanics' Institute looking for money. 'Is the Minister in?' they would say, referring to Jim. I'd see people going into his office, a murmur of words, then hear the rustle of a note and then the hand-over of some money. 'What are you doing that for?' I'd ask him later, but Jim would reply 'nothing, it's not important'. People would come in to him with their ESB bills for him to pay. He wasn't into material things, money wasn't important to him. Jim focused on equality as an issue right through his life, it was one of his abiding passions.

Looking over Jim Kemmy's political career, Joe Wallace told the author that Kemmy experienced considerable changes and transformation during his life:

> He underwent a substantial transition moving from the emphatic socialism that characterised his activism of the 1960s and 1970s to becoming a local cultural icon in the 1990s. This saw him make a contribution that was rooted in local history and culture but saw the early emphatic socialist positions moderated or, some might suggest, abandoned. I see Jim Kemmy as being in the line of previous working class activists such as the nineteenth century labour activist Keir Hardie.[40] He shared many parallels with Hardie being largely self-educated and taking strong and principled stances on social issues which were ahead of their time.

Joe Wallace concluded that it was necessary to view Kemmy's life as a hierarchy of local, national and European activism:

> He was always a committed European, with a strong European perspective. He supported the entry to the EU when the majority of the labour movement opposed entry in 1972. His brother Joe Kemmy remarked to me during the European Parliament elections in 1994 that Jim would have been especially suited to the role of an MEP and I feel he could indeed have made a strong contribution at that level. Thus Jim was essentially a Limerick person but with an outward-looking and even internationalist perspective – something which is in line with the tradition of working class activists like Kier Hardie, Aneurin Bevan[41] or Jim Larkin.[42]

Endnotes

1. *Limerick Leader*, 18 June 1974.
2. *Limerick Leader*, 2 June 1974.
3. *Limerick Leader*, 13 July 1974.
4. *Limerick Leader*, 28 September 1974.
5. *Limerick Leader*, 11 January 1975.
6. *Limerick Leader*, 28 June 1975.
7. *Limerick Leader*, 1975-76.
8. *Limerick Leader*, 7 April 1976.
9. *Limerick Leader*, 13 November 1993.
10. *Limerick Leader*, 24 November 1993.
11. *Limerick Leader*, 15-17 September 1979.
12. *Irish Times*, 16 March 1994.
13. *Limerick Leader*, November 1994.
14. *Limerick Leader*, 4 September 1976.
15. *Limerick Leader*, 15 October 1979.
16. *Limerick Leader*, 16 July 1986.
17. *Limerick Leader* 26 October 1977.

18. *Limerick Leader*, 26 November 1988.

19. *Limerick Leader*, 8 June and 5 October 1988.

20. *Limerick Leader*, 23 July 1994.

21. *Limerick Leader*, 25 February and 11 March 1985.

22. *Limerick Leader*, 8 September 1979.

23. *Limerick Leader*, 22 June 1990.

24. *Limerick Leader*, 12 February 1977.

25. *Limerick Leader*, 10 May 1993.

26. *Limerick Leader*, 18 April 1990.

27. Remember Jim Kemmy (Limerick Gallery of Art, 1999).

28. Kemmy Collection (UL).

29. *Limerick Leader*, 22 June 1992.

30. Kemmy Collection (UL).

31. Kemmy Collection (UL).

32. Kemmy Collection (UL).

33. Mayoral address by Jim Kemmy, Limerick City Council, 3 July 1995.

34. *Limerick Leader*, 5 August 1995.

35. *Irish Times*, 23 August 1995.

36. Kemmy Collection (UL).

37. *Irish Times*, 30 January 1996.

38. Kemmy Collection (UL).

39. *Limerick Leader*, 4 November 1995.

40. Keir Hardie, one of the founders of the British Labour Party in the nineteenth century, was an MP and trade unionist from relatively humble origins.

41. Bevan was one of the leaders in the British Labour Party in the mid-twentieth century, a major social reformer from a coal-mining background.

42. From an impoverished background, Larkin was a founder of the Irish trade union movement and the Labour Party in the early twentieth century.

6

Jim Kemmy – Writer, Publisher, Historian

Kemmy's political work at national and local level was par-
alleled by his emerging career as a writer and publisher,
complementing and reinforcing this work through a series of
journals and publications.

In 1972, following his departure from the Labour Party,
Kemmy established the 'Limerick Socialist Organisation',
aiming to promote socialist ideas in the locality. One of the
immediate actions by the group was the publication of a periodical entitled the *Limerick Socialist*, a monthly newsletter
providing an alternative viewpoint to the dominant discourse
of the mainstream media.[1] Kemmy believed that this could
be a groundbreaking publication. He viewed the established
provincial newspapers as being conservative, and serving as
'capitalist propaganda', avoiding publishing material considered unpalatable or challenging to the general consensus.
Kemmy believed that commercial considerations severely
limited the editorial freedom of the mainstream media, and
that an alternative socialist publication, not shackled by such
constraints, could make a valuable contribution.[2]

The *Limerick Socialist* was published monthly between 1972 and 1981, with over 100 issues, selling about 1,000 copies per issue. Many of its articles were not attributed to authors to avoid the dangers of the libel legislation, and were focused on three main themes: politics, local issues and the arts. Kemmy saw it as a socialist newspaper giving socialist views, aiming to expose hypocrisy and abuses, highlighting the societal failures of the class system. Satire and humour were used actively by the *Limerick Socialist*, aiming to ridicule and caricature its targets.

The local issues highlighted over the years in the *Limerick Socialist* provide good illustrations of Kemmy's approach.

In the first edition of the newsletter, Kemmy targeted a specific confectioner who had criticised the poor reliability of Limerick workers. Kemmy's article retorted with details of the confectioner's business – non-unionised with little training going on – calling for trade union action against him. The same edition castigated the condition of roads in working-class neighbourhoods, arguing that the City Council budgets were more concentrated on wealthier parts of the city.

In the second edition, Kemmy focused on a named Limerick businessman and his difficulties with insurance. In a separate article, he reported excessive profits by the local butchers, and their reluctance to use the official abattoir as required by public regulations.

Also in 1972, he attacked the 'Confraternity', a religious association promoted by the Redemptorist priests, as being 'notorious for its fanatical and demented type of religion'. In the same issue, an article praised workers at the German-owned Krups company for their industrial action in favour of an improved wage agreement. In the same year, the *Limerick Socialist* profiled an eviction by a landlord in the city, claiming references in the local mainstream media had 'whitewashed' the affair and hid the distress suffered by the tenants involved.

A local priest's call for women to stay at home was ridiculed as ignoring economic realities. Support for local authority tenants' causes by the *Limerick Leader* was satirised as 'humbug' and self-serving. The closure of the fee-paying Crescent College ended many years of 'privilege and snobbery . . . having consciously served a small, corrupt, back-scratching clique of local businessmen', according to Kemmy. Later in 1972, the *Limerick Socialist* attacked what it called the 'bonanza' arising from the award of funds to a private hospital by the Mid Western Health Board, with no back-up financial statements to support the decision.

But it was not just the Church and property interests that attracted Kemmy's onslaughts – he tackled the unions too. The *Limerick Socialist* undertook an analysis of the closure in 1972 of the Clover Meats bacon factory, explaining that, while free trade and new working methods brought about the demise of the operation, internal union disputes were also a factor. While other unions were dismantling their closed shops, the pork butchers 'were still entrenched behind their traditions, clinging to a form of trade unionism unsuited to the new situation. The exclusive and clannish nature of their society had resulted in their failure to win the support of their fellow factory workers . . .'

In 1973, an assessment of industrial disputes at the Ferenka plant in Limerick concluded with the call for workers there to organise themselves into a strong, united force and extend the concept of collective bargaining from the bottom upwards, making new demands for industrial democracy. Kemmy also argued against 'closed shops', where employers agreed with a single union to hold negotiating rights in their firm. Kemmy claimed that these arrangements represented a backward step, creating barriers between Irish workers at the behest of employers, and he called for workers to organise together at trade union level.

Kemmy also targeted named individuals in the professions. In one instance, saying that 'the solicitors have the city sewn up', he criticised a prominent Limerick solicitor as epitomising the successful legal operator: 'Wealthy and powerful, he had extended his interests in recent years to business and property undertakings. He also owns a second house in Kilkee.' A Limerick builder was specifically highlighted by name, with Kemmy criticising his 'excessive lifestyle' and 'insatiable hunger for status and recognition'.

In 1974, the *Limerick Socialist* reported a redundancy claim in a Limerick garage, rejected by the employer on the grounds that the employee concerned was retiring early on the grounds of ill-health. Kemmy claimed that this defence was false, and that the financial resources available to the employer were substantially adequate to grant the employee's claim. In the same year, other local controversies were profiled, such as a rent strike in a Southill housing estate and industrial relations conflicts in the SPS company in Shannon.

Few were exempt from Jim Kemmy's fire. The newly established NIHE (National Institute of Higher Education), later to become the University of Limerick, was warned in 1974 about the danger of 'cultural neo-colonialism, teacher-centred education and self-perpetuation into an intellectual prison'. Other targets included the local Limerick newspapers for being 'bloated with advertising fodder and, at the same time, being starved of real news and of being hastily put together with left-over articles, supplied scripts . . . and odds and ends of all sorts'. A Lenten pastoral in 1975 from Bishop Jeremiah Newman was roundly criticised for its 'failure to denounce the materialism of the rich'. Bishop Newman attracted further attention in 1980, having made a historical criticism of the pros-elytising of the Protestant Churches in Ireland of the 1850s, a criticism that, according to the *Limerick Socialist*, 'ignored the equally powerful proselytising forces of the Catholic Church in Africa and Asia'.

Successive mayors drew criticism over the years – Ted Rus-sell, Frank Prendergast, Thady Coughlan, Paddy Kiely and Mick Lipper – although in some cases these verbal attacks, in a poor attempt at satire, degenerated nastily into hurtful per-sonal remarks about their appearance or manner of speech. This was vitriol at its worst.

An article in 1980 detailed a controversy with a local credit union which, reportedly unjustifiably, refused refunds on the closure of an account, until solicitors' letters were issued by the individual concerned. A further article in 1980 explored a controversial RTÉ documentary into working conditions in a County Kerry company, where pressure was reportedly put by the employers on RTÉ to withdraw the programme. The same issue carried a critical review of industrial relations at the Al-can plant in Aughinish, County Limerick. Also in 1980, ac-cusations were levelled at the Moylish Technical College (now Limerick Institute of Technology) on political interference in staff appointments.

Linkages between Limerick and Northern Ireland featured prominently. In 1975, the public outcry against the kidnapping by republicans of Dr. Tiede Herrema, the Dutch chief execu-tive of the Ferenka plant, was contrasted with the silence that followed similar kidnappings of business people in Northern Ireland, exposing the 'vacillating attitudes to the campaign to coerce the Northern Irish Protestant community'. In 1981, a review of Seán South, the Limerick IRA volunteer who died in a 1957 shoot-out in Northern Ireland, concluded that South was a 'grim reminder of hot-house Catholicism and perverted nationalism of the period'.

Most of the reports on local controversies were concentrated in the early years of the *Limerick Socialist*. In the later years of the publication, greater attention was given to national issues, such as Northern Ireland, family planning, Catholic Church, industrial relations and political questions. Also, the newsletter began to give more prominence to historical subjects, especially re-publications of the *Bottom Dog*, a working-class paper in Limerick in 1917-18. This shift possibly reflected Kemmy's growing political maturity, and his emerging interest in national-level issues and local history.

Kemmy was an expert at managing the media. Brendan Halligan of the *Limerick Leader* told the author:

> As a local union and party officer in the late sixties, Jim was a godsend to local media. He knew instinctively how to make news. He focused on issues of public interest. For instance, he prophetically exposed property speculation. He was always prepared to explain himself off the record. On the record, he issued copperplate statements that were trenchant and eye-catching. He helped boost newspaper sales and in so doing increased his political clout. The impact of the *Limerick Socialist* magazine might have surprised many people in Limerick – it didn't surprise me.

Seamus Harrold explained:

> The *Limerick Socialist* was printed by a confidential printer – it was a secret who was doing the printing, the threat of libel or slander was so great, precautions had to be taken. For Jim, the *Limerick Socialist* was a way of having a swipe at people.

The *Limerick Socialist* ceased publication in 1981, replaced by new national-level newsletters of the DSP. In retrospect, while the *Limerick Socialist* could be criticised for its frequently vicious and one-sided attacks on organisations and personalities, and at times was offensively intrusive, it did fulfil some functions of an alternative publication, outside the mainstream, providing a socialist and left-wing perspective on the changing Limerick economy. It gave another view of events, looking at local actors and issues from a different standpoint, generating a strong and controversial commentary. But perhaps the major contribution of the *Limerick Socialist* was that it gave Jim Kemmy the experience and training ground for another, and more durable, publishing initiative.

Around the latter years of the *Limerick Socialist*, Kemmy embarked on this second local venture, one rooted in the historical heritage of Limerick. The Old Limerick Society had originally been founded back in 1943, aiming to promote the study of the history and antiquities of Limerick, continued in existence for some years but dissolved in 1953. Kemmy and a group of local heritage enthusiasts sought to resurrect this society, and take up and expand the work of the 1940s group. In the first edition of the new *Old Limerick Journal*, in December 1979, Kemmy brought his socialist ideas to bear on local history, arguing that the study of 'remarkable' people and events has invariably meant history written from above and conceived in the narrow terms of the ruling families and a self-chosen cultural elite. As a result, high politics and the doings of the rich and powerful occupied the centre of the historical stage through the centuries. The annals of the poor are, by comparison, so brief as to be almost non-existent. The *Old Limerick Journal* sought to redress the balance and open up history in a broad and democratic way.

People without a full and unbiased knowledge of the culture and civilisation of their locality and country are prisoners of history. Local history has long been the province of enthusiasts – some with more enthusiasm than understanding. Most local historians developed and wrote in isolation from their fellows. The new venture aimed to bring the local history enthusiasts in Limerick under one umbrella, charting some of the real-life experiences of Limerick and its people, according to the first edition of the *Old Limerick Journal*.

Seamus Harrold described the background of the *Old Limerick Journal* to the author:

> The year 1974 saw a huge change in Jim's life. In the local elections, I remember vividly the day he called then, I was 18 at the time and had my first vote. He had just been elected to the City Council. The National Monuments Committee (an advisory committee giving advice to the council on care of national monuments in the city, comprising councillors and nominees from heritage groups) had been set up, nobody wanted it, it was of no interest to the other councillors, so Jim got nominated to it, and became chairman. This was exceptional as Jim had been excluded from other committees; he was seen as 'Kemmy the Commie' and the 'red under the bed' (reflecting what people then saw to be his Communist leanings and left-wing extremism).
>
> Other people he met on that committee really transformed his thinking. First there was Kevin Hannon, arch-Catholic, very conservative, right-wing, totally remote from Jim in many ways yet had a passion for the historic buildings and architecture. This fused with Jim's love for stone and the two found common purpose in the built environment and the echoes of history. The second was my mother, Patsy Harrold, active in the Thomond Archaeological Society and enthused for environment

and conservation. Outside the society and the monuments committee, Patsy had little social activity, with six children and my father very sick, so all this brought a welcome outlet. After committee meetings the three often went for drinks together, laying the basis of an active partnership in the years to come.

Seamus Harrold also explained that Jim Kemmy would have been totally hostile at that time to what he saw as the 'upper classes':

> But by 1974 he could see some goodness in them, he started to mix with business people and property owners, bringing a metamorphosis in his life and his outlook. He began to realise that you had to mix with people, even if you did not agree with them, you could respect them if they were doing good work. Jim really brought the National Monuments Committee to life, he engaged with it and transformed it into a force of serious influence in the City Council. He had a love of stone and buildings and met fellow-travellers there, but like Kevin Hannon, they were certainly strange bed-fellows!

The partnership with Kevin Hannon was echoed by Joe Kemmy to the author. Completely different to Kemmy, Hannon, a tailor with Crescent Clothing Ltd., was an ardent Catholic and daily mass-goer, but shared his enthusiasm for old buildings around Limerick:

> This difference was funny at times. Once Kevin accidentally sat in on one of Jim's socialist meetings, and horrified everybody with his right-wing views. 'What on earth is this fellow doing here?' wondered the shocked left-wingers!

Thus were the foundations of the *Old Limerick Journal* laid.

From 1978 to his death in 1997, Jim Kemmy, with Kevin Hannon, Patsy Harrold and others, led the publication as editor of the *Old Limerick Journal*,[3] producing no fewer than 31 issues, with over 600 separate articles: profiles of individual personalities (230) events and happenings (230) and historical descriptions of local places (150). Print runs averaged 1,000 per issue, all sold. What was particularly significant was that the articles were written by as many as 223 separate individuals. While over two-thirds wrote just one article each, a core group of contributors wrote several articles over the life of the journal.

Contributors were drawn from diverse social backgrounds: workers, technicians, professionals, trade unionists, property owners, employers, religious[4] and others. This was truly a 'festival of writing', mobilising a range of local activists to develop and share their enthusiasm for the history and heritage of Limerick. A typical issue would incorporate 40 pages, with 10-15 different articles. Over the years, the *Old Limerick Journal* grew in ambition, producing five large-scale special editions in the late 1980s and 1990s, each with 150+ pages and over 30 Limerick-focused articles: Barrington Family, the Famine, Siege of Limerick, French Revolution and Australia. Production quality was excellent, with copious illustrations and visuals. Research and finish in the articles were of a high standard, reflecting the strict editorial control imposed by Kemmy and his team.

Kemmy was prolific, writing in each issue, his articles providing a good reflection of the tenor and content of the many contributions.

One story was especially poignant. In 'The Death of a Cabin Boy,' Kemmy recounted the tale of a ship sailing to Limerick in the 1830s. Following a severe storm, all food provisions had been washed overboard. After two weeks, with excruciating hunger, it was decided that one of the crew should be killed to keep the others alive. Lots were drawn, and the cabin boy, Patrick O'Brien, drew the shortest lot. It was later suggested the lottery had been rigged against him. Young O'Brien bravely bared his wrists but, when the veins were cut, the blood refused to flow. Eventually, the cook was compelled to cut the boy's throat. The rest of the story is equally gory, with three other crew members being similarly put to death. The surviving members were later rescued by a passing ship. After their return to Limerick, the captain and crew were tried for murder, but were acquitted. The ship owner, Francis Spaight, a well-known Limerick merchant, made a public appeal for assistance to the survivors, contributing £10 to the support fund.

Other examples of Kemmy's profiling of events included an account of a scuffle in the late nineteenth century between some warring families and the local police, with a siege of a house called the 'siege of Clampett Bow'. Kemmy adroitly used the newspapers of those times (*Limerick Chronicle*, 1881) to illustrate the conflicts of local society:

> It would appear that the Irishtown and Englishtown have relapsed into their former disorderly state, more particularly the former, for on Sunday evening and night it was the arena of a series of turbulent scenes enacted by the more depraved portion of the inhabitants there such as to defy description. Clare Street station remains still short of its full complement of constables . . . and taking advantage of the paucity of the force, the rowdies of the locality have matters all their own way, culminating in scenes of turbulence and rioting on Sunday night that would disgrace Indian savages.

Kemmy's trade union background gave him extensive resources for his historical writings on several topics, such as the 'Park Danes' – agricultural workers in the nineteenth century, hired and employed by the day, with insecure livelihoods, living in rudimentary and poor accommodation: 'The system was the Irish version of the slave trade and was riddled with class distinction.'

A further feature highlighted stone and stonemasons in Limerick, showing how the continuity of stonecutting and building throughout the nineteenth century gave Limerick a strong tradition of expert masons and stonecutters. Kemmy wrote how Limerick rests on a bedrock of limestone and it was only natural that architects should turn to the abundant supply of this indigenous local material when it came to the design of new buildings. Limerick limestone earned a wide reputation for its quality and general attractiveness and was also exported to London. Associated with this asset, Limerick stonecutters and masons were first-class tradesmen, according to Kemmy:

> The masons had a secret language of their own called *bearlagar na saor*. When I started my own apprenticeship to the trade, in the early the 1950s, bits of the language were still spoken by some of the old masons. The general form and grammatical structure was that of Gaelic in most parts of Ireland, but the masons in the English-speaking parts used an English framework. The vocabulary also contained many words from a variety of other languages.

Kemmy's interest in workers and labourers was reflected too in a piece on 150 years of Irish railway in which he accurately assessed the social context:

> A rigid hierarchy of seniority operated among the drivers, starting with the passenger train drivers, followed by the 'special' or excursion men and goods train drivers. The last two grades were the pilot men who did the shunt-

ing work and the shed-turners who worked in the loco yard and station. The coming of the diesel and electric trains brought the steam age and these demarcations to an end.

This enthusiasm for labour history led Kemmy to write about the 'Limerick Soviet', a colourful story from Ireland's war of independence. Following a shoot-out in 1919 between Irish volunteers and police constables, the British army declared Limerick to be a Special Military Area, demanding permits from all who left or entered the city, effectively putting the city under permanent curfew. In response, a general strike was called by the Limerick labour movement, organised by a committee declaring itself to be a 'soviet' (i.e. a self-governing committee). Troops were boycotted, money was printed by the strike committee, special newspapers were published and food prices were controlled. Shopkeepers collaborated in the protest. The city-wide strike lasted for two weeks, but was then suspended – it was not something that could have been sustained for any lengthy period. For Kemmy, this would have been a good example of the hidden labour element in Ireland's history, subsequently overshadowed by nationalism. Kemmy wrote frequently about Limerick's first working class paper, the *Bottom Dog*, a weekly publication written and circulated by some of the leaders of the Trades Council and continued for 48 editions to November 1918.

Social practices were featured when Kemmy reminisced about 'packet and tripe', a local Limerick dish, part of the sheep's belly with pudding, a traditional food in Limerick from the nineteenth century:

Until about a decade ago Limerick was the centre of the country's bacon curing industry. This position was reflected in many ways in the life of the city, particularly in its food. During the depressed times of the thirties, forties and fifties, 'bones' of all shapes and descriptions – back-bones, eyebones, breastbones, spare ribs, strips, lots and knuckles – were familiar sights on the kitchen tables of those working class families fortunate enough to be able to afford them. Pig's heads, tails toes (crubeens), sheeps heads and feet (trotters), were also eagerly devoured in many homes.

But perhaps not something for twenty-first century palates!

In focusing on places, Kemmy drew attention to several, often unknown, corners of Limerick such as 'Billy Carr's garden', a cultivated area in the centre of Limerick traced to a local landowner, according to sources at the time:

> The garden of Mr William Carr was famous at this period for its beauty and was cultivated in the first style by an experienced gardener. Mr Carr had three sisters who generally walked each day in the garden dressed in white in the fashion of the time, with large gold watches displayed.

The garden also featured in a local song:

> You may travel the nation all over,
> From Dublin to sweet Mullingar,
> And a garden you will not discover
> Like the garden of sweet Billy Carr.

Roches' hanging gardens were roof gardens, built over stores, by the local merchant William Roche in the early eighteenth century:

> In 1808 William Roche built large stores . . . on the roof of these stores he constructed his own private gardens . . . the top terraces contained hot houses, conservatories, glass houses, and flues to heat them . . . in the middle tier were grown vegetables and hardy fruit trees . . . on the bottom, flowers . . . the depth of earth averaged about five feet and

the stores underneath were protected from dampness by flags cemented together.

A further locality was pinpointed:

Most of us take the name of Garryowen very much for granted. We know that a famous military air, a senior rugby team, and a few other sporting groups have been called after it.

Owen's garden, the origins of Garryowen, represented two Irish words signifying a plot owned by an Owen, well known as a rendezvous point for young people. Shanny's pub, where three sisters (Kate, Mary and Ann) of a family of fishermen and market gardeners kept a bar at Plassey, a regular rendezvous for fishermen and anglers, generating a wealth of anonymous poetry:

I oft time think as my days draw nigh
Of a pub near Plassey mill
Of a field and hedge, all blossom stared
Where the anglers drank at will;
And when the dark would shroud the scene,
Hushing the merry din,
Ann Shanny would look around and ask:
'Well boys, are ye coming in?'

Kemmy put the spotlight on individuals from a range of backgrounds and periods, but all representing people from everyday life, illustrating the social conditions of their time.
'Josie' was a Limerick beggar:

A life-long and dedicated 'drop-out', ever before the term had become fashionable or had even been invented. . . . A stocky man of indeterminate age who wore the same distinctive uniform winter and summer: an old, shiny cap pulled well down over the neatly shaped head; a thick scarf smothering the neck; a long, black overcoat, tied in the middle like a Franciscan's robe, covering an indefinite number of shorter coats. . . . A battered pipe going full steam. . . . A fixed averted stare. . . . A quiet metallic voice. . . . A pair of woollen socks, tucked tightly into heavy boots. . . . A stout walking stick, held sergeant-major style, permanently under the left arm. . . . Put all these, and a few more images together and a picture of Josie comes into focus . . . he never compromised his life-long refusal to participate in the economic competition of society.

One colourful Limerick character of the 1930s, 'carman' at the dockside and vegetable supplier was profiled humorously:

One of the best-known of Limerick's many characters of fifty years ago was James 'Doggy' Cross. The leading member of the Arch-Confraternity[5] of his day, Doggy was renowned for his passionate – and sometimes violent – love of the Pope and the Redemptorist Fathers. His ebullient exploits and colourful stories still told about him are now a familiar part of Limerick folklore . . . after the members (of the Arch-Confraternity) had been stirred up (in 1904) by an anti-Semitic sermon, Doggy was making his way home . . . as an old bearded Jew trotted along the footpath, Doggy lashed out and capsized him. 'Why did you do that to me? I did nothing to you,' queried the plaintive victim. 'Ye crucified Christ,' shouted the enraged Doggy. 'But that happened two thousand years ago,' protested the flattened Jew. 'Makes no difference,' replied his towering protagonist, 'I only heard about it tonight.'

P.J. Ryan was involved in the Free State army during the civil war, and wrote a manuscript entitled *The Fourth Siege of Limerick*, an account of the war of independence and civil war in the city. Kemmy described how Ryan set the military history in the context of the social conditions at the time, particularly the gap between rich and poor, illustrating Ryan's graphic writing style:

> In setting the scene for the Civil War, he give a hitherto unexplored view of Georgian Limerick from the depths of the city sewers. His description of bewigged and buckled servants elegantly tipping brimming chamber pots into the mouths of sewers named Cornwallis, Victoria and George every morning is vivid and colourful.

Delightful.

Kemmy wrote an extensive analysis of Kate O'Brien, the Limerick-born novelist, exploring how the experiences of Kate O'Brien in her teenage years in the city forged her approach to writing. With admiration for O'Brien's social insights, he quoted her extensively when she wrote about a fictional town that represented Limerick of the nineteenth century:

> The crumbling old town that looked so gently beautiful at evening, grey, sad, and tender, huddled on humpy bridges over canals and twisting streams . . . under its mask of dying peace it lived a swarming, desperate, full-blooded life, a life rich in dereliction, the life of beggars, drunkards, idiots, tramps, tinkers, cripples, a merry cunning, ribald, un-protesting life of despair and mirth and waste.

That alternative view of Irish communities, highlighting what he saw as the inequalities and the injustices, was forever accurate for Kemmy.

Other historical personalities examined by Kemmy included James Roche, Limerick merchant caught up in the revolution in France in the 1790s. Born in Limerick, Roche had been living in Bordeaux at the time of the revolution, meeting Dr. Guillotine, the inventor of the death machine that was to bear his name. Guillotine was a teacher at the time: 'He was occupied about heads in a different way from that which afterwards obtained his attention,' according to Roche. Another French connection was George Bennis, also from Limerick, a publisher in the 1800s: 'George Bennis was to feature in a sensational drama in France. During one of the several attempted assassinations of King Louis Philippe, he saved the life of the monarch and was awarded the title of Chevelier,' wrote Kemmy.

He reviewed 'Feathery Bourke' a Limerick merchant who died in 1973, describing his personality and business in the city, mostly from ground rents and scrap metal. Although without formal education, Bourke had an uncanny knowledge of property and related business issues. He was an 'emperor of ground rents,' according to Kemmy, writing with some grudging respect. Businessmen make poor revolutionaries and Feathery Bourke was no exception to this rule, taking steps to ensure his economic survival:

> In the early nineteen-twenties the Black and Tans set fire to three houses owned by the Bourkes in Cornmarket Row. During the fire, Feathery's mother, Lil, rushed into the burning building and later emerged tightly clutching two pillow-cases stuffed with money. It was during this period also that Feathery pulled off one of his biggest business coups. The Strand Barracks had served as a base for the British military forces, and during the Civil War it had been occupied by republican forces. After the war, the Barracks was put up on the market for sale, and despite some intimidation by local nationalist forces, Feathery attended the sale and bought the property for a proverbial 'song'. He later sold the Barracks to the Limerick Corporation at a big profit.

Kemmy summed him up thus: 'Bourke would make Scrooge look like Santa Claus.'

The Siege of Limerick also provided ample scope for individual profiles, such as Peter Drake, a nineteen-year-old at the time who left Limerick after the siege and later published his personal memoirs of life in Europe. Drake was apparently a colourful character, serving as a solder of fortune separately for four countries in the Dutch, Spanish, French and British forces. His memoirs, *Amiable Renegade*, were for his family too candid with the result that they suppressed the book by buying up all available copies: 'They objected to the book's revelations and frankness.' But this attempt was unsuccessful as several copies survived, and the book went on to become a serious collector's item. Reflecting the *Old Limerick Journal's* interest in people on the margin, Kemmy concluded:

> For all his passion for wine, women and gambling, Peter Drake was an intelligent and courageous man. He was a wayward wild goose, and his book is a most valuable account of the life of one Irish soldier who left Limerick in 1691.

Another international story was that of Martin Cherry, a Limerick man in Australia, unwillingly taken as a hostage by the Kelly gang of outlaws, the 'bushrangers'. In the midst of a shoot-out between the Kelly gang and the police, Cherry was accidentally killed by a stray police bullet, something that the police first denied but later admitted under pressure from an investigating commission: 'Criticism of the conduct of the police during the Kelly hunt has continued to reverberate through Australian history to this day,' wrote Kemmy, reflecting his sympathy for anybody inadvertently suffering at the hands of the law enforcers.

There were also several reviews of poets and dramatists, such as Michael Hogan, the 'Bard of Thomond', who had 'lampooned members of the Limerick Corporation, the Catholic bishop, the merchant princes and professional people and had

brought himself notoriety and unpopularity'. Also highlighted was the contribution of other writers, such as John Francis O'Donnell. In fact, O'Donnell and Hogan had no liking
for each other, a particularly bitter relationship, with Kemmy
quoting these nasty lines written by O'Donnell about Hogan:

I knew him well; keen witted sly,
Thin lipped, with an eternal sneer
Wreathing his mouth; a lustrous eye,
Deep, passionate, but insincere.

Man of all moods; a misanthrope
At least in brain if not in heart -
His sole ambition – his one hope
To hurl the lance or shoot the dart.

Evidently, poets in those days were best not offended!

Kemmy successfully exploited the *Old Limerick Journal* to
highlight issues in the development and change in Limerick.
For example, writing about Cannock's Clock, a prominent
landmark on top of the then Cannock's store:

The sight of the clock tower, high above the eastern end
of O'Connell street, gave re-assurance and confidence in
troubled times: its familiar chimes ringing out over the
city brought the tidings of time to citizens young and old.
Earlier this year the replacement of the city's best known
clock by a brash, brightly coloured Disneyland-type time-
piece caused widespread concern.

But developments at the Granary, an eighteenth century
warehouse and grain store, attracted more favourable comment. This, according to Kemmy, was an example of the industrial architecture of Limerick City, restored as an urban
renewal feature in the 1980s:

It is a fine example of the industrial architecture of Georgian Limerick. The restored building shows how an old structure can be imaginatively adapted for modern, functional use. In today's new world of concrete and glass, the Granary has given physical expression and real meaning to urban renewal in Limerick.

Kemmy also wrote in its praise with some poetic licence:

Brick upon brick, stone upon stone
The grain store was built in 1787
By the workers of Limerick
For Philip Roche, a merchant prince . . .

. . . Come, let us go into the tavern
And drink a toast to
Brick and stone, grain and grog
And to all who laboured here.

Kemmy's writing style matured over the years, extending in scope and growing in precision and detail. Significantly, from his evolving historical perspective, he developed a sympathy and balance in his analysis of major Limerick business families of previous generations, a sympathy that was in sharp contrast to the earlier virulence and antagonism of the *Limerick Socialist*. His profile of Arthur's Quay acknowledged the contribution of the prominent Arthur family in Limerick in the late 1700s: 'For about 500 years, the Arthurs were one of the most prominent families in Limerick . . . merchants, members of the professions, administrators, clergymen and holders of public office such as mayor and sheriff.'

Later, Kemmy wrote about the development of Barringtons Hospital in the 1830s, with interesting anecdotes, including how the opening of Barringtons was delayed by hostilities between two surgeons among the hospital staff. Apparently, one surgeon took grievous exception to the appointment of the other. The result was an altercation in the street and violence with sticks, followed by a lengthy court case.

In an assessment of housing and social conditions at the time, Kemmy wrote:

> The insanitary lanes, with their open sewers and rows of overcrowded cabins, were the causes of much ill-health, and the Limerick Corporation and local health authority met with little success in tackling the problems of the slums, and were content to allow charitable bodies and the hospitals to deal with the results of the squalor rather than redress the source of the problem. The wretched living conditions of the poor were taken for granted, and few houses were built by the public authorities until well into the present day.

There was also a piece about the Tait family, major clothing producers in Limerick, with business connections with the United States and Australia. The rise of Peter Tait, the founder, was well described as an entrepreneurial example:

> He secured employment as a shop assistant . . . during a recession in trade, Peter Tait was laid off work, but he did not allow this misfortune to daunt him. Instead he seized on the opportunity to show the initiative and character to take him to the top of the industrial world. He purchased a hawker's basket, stocked it with wares, which he sold in the city and to sailors from visiting sailing ships. After long months at sea, the sailors were among his best customers . . . Tait soon realised the potential of his expanding market . . . he became an employer . . . three years later he was advertising for 500 shirt makers.

Tait subsequently went on to become an international merchant, supplying uniforms to the British and confederate American armies.

Kemmy was also successful in linking the big national stories of historical periods with Limerick, thus giving major controversies a strong local resonance. For example, writing about the Irish famine of the nineteenth century:

> It has frequently been recorded that Limerick escaped the worst rigours of the famine, but, as the contents of this publication will show, this is far too simplistic a conclusion. The famine caused unprecedented death, misery and emigration in Limerick as elsewhere. There was also a large influx of desperate, poverty-stricken people to the city from the surrounding counties, particularly Clare, and many of them perished in transition. This publication tells the story, in all its horrors, of the famine in Limerick from 1845 to the 1850s. It is an attempt to confront and explain what happened in the city and county during this dreadful period.

This approach to big events was also in evidence in a special edition about the Siege of Limerick where Kemmy wrote: 'The sieges of Limerick in 1690 and of Derry in 1689 were important milestones in Irish history, but their defensive legacy bred and nurtured a siege mentality that has all too often prevailed in Irish life, north and south. We must not remain prisoners of our history.'

As a historical analyst, Kemmy was fascinated by the 'historiography' of Limerick, charting how different historians had looked at the city from time to time, pinpointing the contribution of different writers:

> The two best known histories of Limerick were written by John Ferrar and Maurice Lenihan. A third major history, written by Reverend Patrick Fitzgerald and John James McGregor, has not received the same attention as the other two works . . . for too long their work has been overshadowed by the histories of Ferrar and Lenihan. A

study of Fitzgerald and McGregor will repay the reader by providing much valuable information about Limerick and its people.

Kemmy's adept ability to analyse was typified in a tribute to Kevin Danaher, Irish folklorist, in this sharp assessment of the meaning of folklore:

> Folklore is often regarded as a lesser but harmless branch of history, or as mere fireside storytelling in thatched cottages in rural Ireland. To treat the subject in this condescending way is to misunderstand the value of folklore. Folklore is not a licence to invent or embellish history; it is the people's lore – the distillation of the everyday experiences of the generality of men and women. It combines the study of work and play of the ordinary people and the influences of their lives of custom, tradition and religion. And, contrary to the widely held belief in Ireland, folklore embraces both urban and rural life.

Perhaps this last quote neatly encapsulates Kemmy's entire philosophy in driving the *Old Limerick Journal*.

'Jim Kemmy's interest in local history came from his labour and trade union background – he was very interested in local characters,' reported Joe Kemmy. Kemmy threw himself into the *Old Limerick Journal* with passion, devoting countless hours to proofreading and editing, frequently checking scripts in the middle of trade union or political meetings, often to the frustration of other participants. Trade unionist Foncie McCoy told the author:

> Jim Kemmy used to drive us all mad during trade union meetings, busily with his head down checking drafts of his *Old Limerick Journal* or *Limerick Socialist*, in the middle of heavy union discussions. 'Yes, I'm listening,' he would say when we checked if he was conscious of the meeting!

Kemmy was a strict editor, never accepting inadequate material, and meticulous in his corrections and adjustments to articles. 'Perhaps he was conscious of his own lack of formal education, and maybe was compensating for it in this way,' said Margaret O'Donoghue. 'Although many prospective contributors were unable to cope with Jim's stringent editing, he would not tolerate anything he felt was less than excellent,' agreed Patsy Harrold.

Everybody got involved. Dick Spring even told the author how Jim Kemmy would be proof-reading the *Old Limerick Journal* at party meetings in Dublin:

> I would be sucked in to help him with the edits and corrections, we had a shared passion for history and heritage. A further contact was that, via rugby connections, I was a good friend of Kevin Hannon, the co-editor of the *Old Limerick Journal*. Jim might have been better off as a writer and a tradesman, trade unionist also, not a politician, maybe his political commitments deprived Ireland of a great writer. He was a dedicated reader. My memory is of Jim grabbing a pile of books to disappear into maybe a mobile home somewhere in West Clare.

Seamus Harrold confirmed all this:

> The *Old Limerick Journal* was huge work. Jim would spend 24 hours going over the editing, proof-reading thoroughly, punctuation, grammar, everything – it used to drive Patsy mad, him staying up all night!

Another example quoted by Seamus Harrold was that, after the loss of his Dáil seat in 1982, Kemmy immediately withdrew to the comfort zone of the *Journal*, throwing himself into the preparation of yet another edition.

Kemmy's commitment to the *Old Limerick Journal* grew out his passion for books. Niall Greene of the Labour Party told the author how he first met Jim Kemmy at the 1968 by-election, campaigning for the seat following the death of Donagh O'Malley: 'Jim was bursting with energy, bringing me up to his house in Garryowen showing me his massive collection of books, Jim was always lending books, borrowing books, discussing with everybody books of every type and description. Such was the foundation for the *Old Limerick Journal*.

Anna-Maria Hajba told the author:

> Jim Kemmy did not appear to write much in his early years. He certainly spoke a lot in the Dáil and the City Council, and at public meetings, but it seems to be his colleagues in the DSP who produced the policy papers. There is not much evidence in the archives of policy papers being directly written by Kemmy, but he flowered in the many articles in the *Old Limerick Journal*. Maybe his lack of formal education held Kemmy back from writing policy papers. These are difficult to do without academic qualifications, but he may have been more comfortable with the concrete happenings of history, and he went at that with confidence and conviction.

Anna-Maria Hajba concluded:

> The *Old Limerick Journal* seemed to have been a retreat for Jim Kemmy, so much of his existence was wrapped up in politics and trade unions, so the *Old Limerick Journal* was something he could escape into, he could bury himself in history, getting away from the other pressures in his life.

Apart from the *Old Limerick Journal*, Kemmy was also involved in three other significant publications: the *Limerick Anthology*, the *Limerick Compendium* and *Limerick from Old Postcards*.

In advance of the 800th anniversary of Limerick as a chartered city, Jim Kemmy led the publication of the *Limerick Anthology* in 1996. Inspired by John Ferrar,[6] Limerick's first major historian, and Kate O'Brien, the city's most famous novelist, Kemmy reported that, although these two lived almost two centuries apart, they had a common bond of enthusiasm and tolerance in their writings. In the *Anthology*, Kemmy wrote that he tried to emulate the generous and free-wheeling spirit of both. Anthologies, according to Kemmy, should speak for themselves and tell their own stories. What the ideal compilation should aim to achieve is best described by the architectural term 'section through'. As a 'section through' of a detailed drawing is designed to cut inside the façade of a structure to reveal an inner and all-encompassing picture, so should a good anthology – whatever its theme – unfold a wide range of contents and its own distinctive qualities. Rescuing history from oblivion, transmitting remarkable events to posterity, was the call of the historian, argued Kemmy.

The *Anthology* aimed to bring the observations about Limerick of a wide range of historians, poets, writers, travellers and observers, through the centuries, into modern book form. With 170 contributions, in almost 400 pages, the *Anthology* spanned religion, Limerick as a garrison town, land and labour, people, the county, sport, history, drama, the city and stories from travellers. Some of the contributions represented the best from the *Old Limerick Journal*, while others were original contributions, also from local writers, as well as inputs on Limerick from well-known writers from the past, such as Heinrich Böll and Percy French.

At the time of his death in 1997, Kemmy was finalising the *Limerick Compendium*.[7] Complementing the *Anthology*, this was a 400-page collection of Limerick publications, with over 200 separate contributions on similar themes: religion, the military, land, labour, people, county, city, history, drama, politics, fiction and travellers. In the preface, Kemmy reported that literature in Limerick has a long history, going back over 300 years. Publications grew with the development of printing, and the flowering of printers in Limerick provided the basis of many hundreds of books bearing the Limerick imprint, as well as Limerick-related publications outside the city.

Thus over the centuries, poets, historians, novelists and journalists have written about Limerick and its people. Many of their publications have, of course, been published outside the city, mainly in Dublin, London and New York. Given this rich store of literature, the publication of a comprehensive anthology of Limerick writing was long overdue. Indeed, every centre of population should have an updated literary collection in each generation. The work of compiling such a collection provides an opportunity to collect the best out-of-print and not easily available literature, the bulk of which is not worth reprinting.

Also in his last year, Kemmy reproduced in *Limerick from Old Postcards* 140 illustrations from the Limerick City Museum and other sources, featuring Limerick at the dawn of the photographic age, with pictures and supporting text, illustrating prominent buildings like King John's Castle, Barringtons Hospital, Arthur's Quay and St Mary's Cathedral; but also capturing fascinating glimpses of Limerick social life at the turn of the century: brass bands, students, soccer teams, sporting clubs, fire brigade, staff at the bacon factory.[8]

Over the years, the growth and development of Kemmy's local writing emerges clearly in all these publications. The anger and antagonism of the *Limerick Socialist* provided much of his early experience and learning, giving way in time to the more mature, reflective and carefully researched *Old*

Limerick Journal, leading to the substantial achievements of the *Limerick Anthology* and the *Limerick Compendium.* Common in all these writings are the evident attention to detail and insistence on excellence, together with hard work, self-discipline, inquisitive mind and bursting energy, all combined with an absorbing passion for real-life people and their every-day stories.

Endnotes

1. *Limerick Socialist,* 1972-81 (Kemmy Collection, UL).

2. 'Content Analysis of Jim Kemmy's *Limerick Socialist* Publication' by Ciaran O'Doherty (unpublished dissertation, University of Limerick, 2001).

3. *Old Limerick Journal,* 1978-97 (Kemmy Collection, UL).

4. Including Kemmy's old friend and adversary, Bishop Jeremiah Newman. Kemmy never permitted any author to use their official title at the head of their article, but with the sole exception of the Bishop.

5. Religious association in Limerick led by the Redemptorist Fathers.

6. *The Limerick Anthology,* edited by Jim Kemmy (Gill and Macmillan, Dublin, 1996).

7. *The Limerick Compendium,* edited by Jim Kemmy (Gill and Macmillan, Dublin, 1997).

8. *Limerick in Old Postcards,* by Jim Kemmy and Larry Walsh (Zaltbommel European Library, 1997).

7

Jim Kemmy –
Trade Unionist

Kemmy's life as a writer and political activist was comple-mented by his enthusiasm for trade union work, which gave him a rich basis on which to draw insights into the com-ings and goings of people. 'Jim's first love was the trade union work – it absorbed him completely, it was much more impor-tant for him than all the Dublin stuff,' said his friend Patsy Harrold.

Returning from London in the 1960s, Kemmy found him-self working with the chairman of the local branch of the stonemasons' union (also called bricklayers or stonelayers). With a constant flow of new workers onto the building site, there were continuous industrial relations issues which re-quired responses. Jim Kemmy became actively involved in the union at this stage.[1] Within three weeks he was on the branch committee and in three months he became branch secretary. His profile was already significant, with the *Limerick Leader* noting his appointment at the time:

The (stonemasons) society's youngest ever secretary is James Kemmy, and he brings to his work the energy of youth. James, who is with the corporation (city council) maintenance department, was the only provincial delegate from the Union to attend the Congress of Irish Unions in Galway last July. He represents the Union on the Limerick Trades Council, the Apprenticeship Committee, the Delegate Board of the Mechanics Institute and the Area Joint Council for the Building Industry.[2]

The union joined by Kemmy was the local stonemasons' craft union, one union out of many within the system of Irish industrial relations.[3]

Background to Trade Unions

Trade unions have traditionally been seen as the most effective means of countering employer power and achieving satisfactory pay and working conditions for employees. Their role is well established in legislation dating back to the nineteenth century. In essence, trade unions are organisations that aim to unite workers with common interests. The basic strength of a union, therefore, lies in its ability to organise and unite workers – a feature of immense interest to Kemmy with his growing worker consciousness from his London experience.

The early combinations were almost exclusively composed of skilled workers, or 'journeymen' as they were known. They were purely local bodies and their existence was often tenuous.

In the nineteenth century, workers themselves could do little about their situation, as they had weak economic or political power. However, it was only the skilled workers who were successful in establishing any large scale permanent unionisation up to the early twentieth century, such as the craft unions of Kemmy and his colleagues.

Craft unions catered for workers who possessed a particular skill in a trade. Entry was restricted to workers who had completed a prescribed apprenticeship programme. Prominent examples of occupational categories that have been organised in craft unions are electricians and fitters, as well as the stonemasons of Kemmy's union. Craft unions represented the first form of union organisation and had their origins in the early unions that emerged in Britain at the start of the nineteenth century. These 'model' unions, as they became known, confined their membership to skilled categories such as printers and carpenters who had served a recognised apprenticeship in their particular trade.

The early craft unions represented a relatively small proportion of the labour force. In Ireland, it is estimated that by 1890 there were only about 17,500 trade union members in total, all of whom were skilled workers. However the importance of the 'model' unions was that, by becoming accepted as important actors in the industrial relations system, they created a vital bridgehead in ensuring the acceptance of trade unions as part of the political and organisational framework, hence the significance of craft activists like Jim Kemmy.

Craft unions had traditionally been protective of their trade by ensuring that only people holding union cards were permitted to carry out certain types of skilled work. By controlling entry to the craft, such unions customarily held considerable negotiating power. This strategy has often been criticised as being a source of restrictive work practices and demarcation disputes. The relative influence of craft unions has decreased over time, as reflected in the reduction of their share of union membership. Increased mechanisation and consequent de-skilling has also had a detrimental impact on craft union membership, with some older craft unions having ceased to exist as their traditional craft was rendered obsolete by developments in technology and work practices. These were challenges too that would have confronted Jim Kemmy throughout his working life.

The branch is the fundamental element of trade union organisation and provides the means by which the ordinary 'rank and file' can participate directly in the affairs of the union. As the basic unit of trade union organisation, the branch manages the affairs of the union at local level and strives for improvements of the conditions for the branch members, something that would have absorbed much of Kemmy's time in the union.

A unique characteristic of Irish trade unions is the fact that a number of British-based unions have operated in this country, and also that many Irish trade unions owe their origins to British movements. Kemmy's initial experiences with the building unions in London would have exemplified this link.

A common criticism of Irish trade union structure has been that there were too many unions relative to total membership, and that the union system has been one of small and fragmented trade unions. Rationalisation of trade union structure in Ireland has thus been high on the agenda of successive governments, and the promotion of union mergers has long been a trade union objective, another issue for Kemmy's union.

Kemmy drew the development of his ideas from many sources, national and international. For example, in 1967, he was part of a trade union delegation to the Soviet Union marking 50 years of the USSR.[4] At the time, he was reported to be very impressed with the standards of housing and social conditions of the workers.[5] However, subsequent DSP policy papers show a marked dislike for what he saw to be the heavy-handed intervention of the state. It was not the Soviet model, but the liberal tradition of British trade union and labour party socialism, that informed Kemmy's thinking.

The Stonemasons

Kemmy's stonemasons' union owed its origins to a Royal Charter of Charles I for setting down and appointing due rules and orders for 'the arts and mysteries of bricklayers and plasterers around Dublin – also to prevent the evils of unskillfulness of persons who pretend a knowledge of the mysteries'. This was a guild according to the laws of the time. The guild was restricted to the loyal subjects of the King, with the Limerick Brick and Stonemasons' Society being granted a royal charter in 1677. The 'union' was the native craftsmen employed by members of the guild. Combination laws at the time prevented them organising for increasing rates of wages or lessening their hours of work. In time, the union grew and transplanted the guild, which was absorbed in 1840. Plasterers split away and set up a separate union in the 1840s.[6]

The objective of the union, officially called the 'Ancient Guild of Incorporated Brick and Stonelayers and Allied Trades Union', was the organisation of craftsmen in the building industry for the purpose of regulating the rates of pay, hours of work and other conditions of employment and generally advancing the quality of their working lives. Membership was for persons who were qualified as craftsmen in a building trade (or other recognised allied trade), including apprentices. No employer could be a member.

This is a good example of how craft unions owed much of their origin to the guilds of the middle ages and, like the guilds, embraced a wide range of activities for their members – not just representation as in the modern trade unions, but also recruitment, training and setting of standards, functions that have since transferred to other institutions, with the later merger of the crafts into the wide trade union movement.

The National Executive Council of the union had the full powers of government in all its affairs, including control of funds and supervision of full-time officials. Membership was organised into geographical branches, each with a minimum of 12 members. Branches carried on the business of the union in their area, including protection and promotion of the interests of the members, and recruitment of suitably qualified members. Stonelayers were one of the officially recognised craft unions. Under the Industrial Relations Act, 1946, the union made agreements with employers on wages and conditions of employment. The Trade Disputes Act, 1906, was also a major legal framework.

Jim Kemmy was secretary of the Limerick branch, bringing his socialist ideas into the mainstream of the trade union movement, as illustrated in a talk he gave in Limerick around this time:

> The true definition of industrial democracy is the extension of the democratic principle to the workplace. The operation of this form of industrial democracy would bring all the decisions of the work process directly into the responsibility of those involved in the work itself, and would thus establish a full democracy in industry, with shared and cooperative decision-making at all levels. Workers leave democracy at the factory gate when they clock in, and return to it when they clock out.[7]

This early speech by Kemmy was very much in the 'industrial democracy' tradition, a movement that seeks to involve workers in making decisions, sharing responsibility and exercising authority in the workplace. Much of this thinking has already become established in legislation in several countries, such as worker participation in boards of directors. Even among management and business writers, industrial democracy has been cited as a potential boost to productivity and competitiveness. So Kemmy's embracing of the industrial democracy theme had good foundations in both theory and practice, and presaged further developments of those ideas in the years to come. He actively promoted these ideas of industrial democracy within the union movement.

Joe Kemmy reported:

> Jim Kemmy had joined the stonemasons union in London. On his return he saw it was not well organised in Limerick. At the time, he had no electoral ambitions, but focused on the need for workers to organise themselves.

This was confirmed by others:

> Jim Kemmy brought back from London an understanding of poverty and inequality, something occurred in Jim Kemmy's mind in London that gave him a new consciousness about inequality. Back in Limerick, he saw that the local craft unions were protective, closed shops; only the son of a stonemason could get in, occasionally a nephew; anger and indignation came together in his work for the stone masons.[8]

During his work as local secretary, Kemmy worked to advance the masons' aims, particularly catering for the 100 members of the Limerick branch. Three major themes focused his attention: promoting his members' interests in dealing with employers, maintaining a unified approach shared by the different members and groups within the labour movement, and working with the apprenticeship system.

Supporting Union Members

According to Pat Reeves, a key issue for people like Kemmy was that most of the unions were small local groups and that the masons were not well organised:

> The craft unions were more an urban phenomenon, in the rural areas, there was little or no union activity, but there would be families of craftsmen who would be gen-

erally recognised. Jim Kemmy really put his print on it, especially when Shannon industrial estate started in the 1960s. Masons were highly sought-after with the building boom in the 1960s, and the surge in demand. They brought the terms and conditions of work from Limerick to Shannon, which were better than in Clare or Ennis. Ennis had lower rates of pay than Limerick, masons were not organised there. Jim was one of those who ensured that Limerick rates of pay applied in Shannon, not those of Ennis.

Shop stewards, according to Kemmy, were the life blood of union activities. At workplace level, the shop steward is the key union representative and their role is to represent employee interests on workplace issues. In practice, shop stewards may become involved in workplace bargaining involving local grievance and disputes. The shop steward performs a number of important tasks, including recruitment of new union members, collecting union subscriptions, negotiating with management representatives, acting as a channel of communication with union central offices and defending the interests of members. Shop stewards have a difficult situation in that they have to maintain the support of their members while at the same time maintaining a position with management from which they can negotiate effectively.

From Kemmy's perspective, how to properly organise shop stewards was seen to be the key problem. Employers and trade unions should have agreement on the proper organisation of shop stewards on site. Employers should have jobs properly organised and should settle disputes before they arise. Trade unions should have a proper method of checking the cards and operation on the job. The right system should be that the shop steward was an appointee of the trade union. Management should accept this and, where the job is big enough, facilities should be offered to allow the shop steward to operate in a full and free manner.

Several examples from the Kemmy Collection in the University of Limerick illustrate the work of Kemmy and the stonemasons' union at this time.

A controversy erupted with Portland Estates (Limerick building company) in 1968 about workers taking a shorter lunch-break and not going home during lunch hour. Pat Reeves told the author:

> But Portland Estates had to bring in the half-hour rule. Before that, building workers could go home for lunch for one hour, usually by bicycle, but with the expansion of Limerick into the outer suburbs this obviously became impractical and disruptive, so Jim Kemmy accepted it eventually'

In the same years, there was a dispute with the Condensed Milk Company over building craftsmen.

Frequently, particularly during the high inflation years of the 1970s, there were feelings of frustration by members at their wages losing value. If prices were not kept at a reasonable level, they felt the national wage agreement was an unfair means of curbing workers' earnings.

At one stage, in 1978, a meeting of Limerick City Council maintenance craftsmen heard that the Council was awarding contracts without consultation with the craftsmen's union. For example, the Council had given the contract for the building of new toilets at King John's castle to a contractor. The group had reason to believe that most of this work had been done by non-union labour. Observers had seen a handyman doing work that should be done by a mason. The man was not in a union and was later seen working as a labourer. They hoped this was a once-off issue. Discussion had been with the mayor as the contractor was not available. This issue of non-craft workers doing craft work was a perennial source of tension. On one of the social employment schemes of Limerick City Council, Kemmy argued that there should be a clear distinction between craftsmen doing craft work and non-craftsmen doing non-craft work. The officials reported that they had difficulty finding craftsmen. Kemmy claimed in response that they should hire craft apprentices, who could be found easily, he believed.

In another incident members of the union were asked by an employer to carry out particular work on a building site in 1981. They refused as there was an agreed rate for this kind of work, with a bonus agreement, and this was not being applied in this case. Men were suspended but the union negotiated with the company and reached agreement on a special rate.

A dispute between Kemmy's union and McInerney Builders in 1982 occurred over rules of holiday pay, with the union accusing McInerney of exploiting high unemployment to claw back on conditions of employment which had been conceded by the employer in better times when labour had more bargaining power. McInerney had sought to pay holiday pay at less per hour than normal working pay.

Kemmy wrote strongly to a local builder in 1983 noting that they were employing a 'labour only sub-contractor for bricklaying contrary to the registered agreement with the construction industry'. An official dispute was threatened by Kemmy unless the firm terminated this sub-contract arrangement.

With national economic difficulties dominating in 1984, as much as 40 per cent of union members were unemployed. There were an unprecedented number of industrial disputes, many about the use of non-union labour, while other issues were about wages and conditions of employment.

Jim Kemmy argued in 1985 that pay in the construction industry was a 'major scandal' and had fallen seriously out of line with comparable employment elsewhere.

A dispute against Telecom Éireann in 1986 resulted in a 'flying picket', with a picket being reinforced by building workers from across Limerick taking turns at manning the line. 'We closed down Telecom for a week, and they gave in,' reported Joe Kemmy, 'although we could not have kept it up for longer than that.'

Strike notice was served on Limerick City Council in 1987 against work on cobblelock being carried out by contract. Laying of paving brick was regarded as a skilled job done by bricklayers, not by unskilled or semi-skilled workers. There was unemployment among bricklayers but contractors were not using skilled bricklayers. The union believed that the Council did not have an unqualified right to use sub-contractors. In an undated note, Limerick City Council officials reported that they necessarily entered into contracts on a regular basis. But, on no less than 15 occasions, this was challenged by Kemmy and the trade unions in areas such as re-development of John's Castle, laying of sewers, street works and other construction. In the view of the officials, the principal underlying reason for the unions' position was that placing of work capable of being done by direct labour would diminish the amount of available work and money of their members. The continued employment of Council staff would be at risk, Kemmy and his group believed, according to the officials.

Employees were laid off by one employer in 1993 without redundancy payments. Kemmy's union reported that they could bring this to the Employment Appeals Tribunal, but would not do so if there was a realistic proposal to pay them within the next few weeks.

According to Foncie McCoy:

Jim Kemmy was very fiery in the early days. Once there was talk about a five day week, replacing the five and a half day week, but we wanted to maintain the numbers of hours worked the same. So our members were instructed to remain on the building sites until the hours were used up, even though work had ceased. Jim was a real leader at this and was working at a building site, insisted on staying after the site was closed – the builder had to call the Gardaí to remove him on the grounds of trespass.

While conflict was a prominent feature of the stonemasons' union, there was also evidence of bargaining, consensus-building, and ongoing collaboration with employers, a good example being Kemmy's work in the 'Joint Area Council'. According to Joe O'Brien of the Construction Industry Federation:

The Limerick Joint Area Council was a forum where the employers and unions could get together on a regular basis. It provided a very useful vehicle to exchange views and information, but most important in heading off potential conflicts before they became difficult. As the union representative, Jim Kemmy was joint chairman (together with an employer), meeting every two months, but more often if there was a problem to be tackled. In fairness, Jim always took a very responsible approach at these meetings although of course he could be very difficult at times if there was a really big issue. There would obviously be meetings that were very 'robust', to put it mildly – you could be at it hot and heavy for two hours, but afterwards differences were left behind and stayed in the meeting room. When he wanted to be, Jim could be a very tough negotiator. But at the end of the day, he always took the side of what he saw to be 'right'; you could see his social conscience coming out a lot.

Joe O'Brien continued:

In his capacity of joint chairman he would be invited to the annual dinner dance of the Mid West Construction Industry Federation – socially he mixed well with the employers, he was good 'craic' and very jovial, although I noticed he was much more formal and official in his role as TD, in public meetings or on television, but with us he was very informal and friendly. In that context, when he became a TD, we would also meet him regularly in his political role on developing the construction industry in Limerick – he was very helpful and was obviously all powered up about improving the Limerick economy.

I first met Jim when I started with the Construction Industry Federation in 1979. Jim was secretary of the Limerick Building Trades Group at the time, so we had regular contact through periodic meetings. My first impression was the sheer physical size of the man, and his loud booming voice, also significant was the sincerity about him, there was sincerity in his voice, he knew what he was on about. When Jim approached you about a problem or something, you knew there was a real problem there, he would always have done his homework before approaching you, he would never bring in an issue to the meeting based on rumour or hearsay, he would always have checked it out. He was not just passing on complaints, he would have established the facts first, so that meant you always had to listen to him.

Dan Miller explained to the author:

Jim always took the view that if you had a strike you had failed, he tried to find practical solutions to problems at the time. If you wanted to be a successful trade union official, you had to bring your people with you. As a full-time official, you had inevitable influence over people and you had an advantage over them, so you had to respect that. In the event of a serious dispute leading up to a strike, you had to be sure your members really wanted it, and you had to be sure you could win. People working on building sites wanted to make a living and take care of their families, so there was rarely any appetite for strikes. And, on the other side, employers were prepared to settle for the sake of industrial peace.

Foncie McCoy told the author about the day-to-day life of the union officials like Jim Kemmy: 'We would go onto a building site, each of us would see our own people, masons, painters or whatever, checking how people were getting on, had people paid up their dues, were there non-union people doing union work, we would encourage people to join the unions.'

Kemmy's growing ability to bring together different groups in conflict was further recognised in 1995 by correspondence from the Construction Industry Federation. At that time, a controversy arose between the plasterers' union and the Federation, with lightening strikes by plasterers on a major city building site objecting to the use of sub-contract plasterers. Kemmy had acted as a mediator between the two sides, acknowledged by a letter to Kemmy from the Federation: 'I would like to take the opportunity of thanking you for your assistance in chairing the meeting in such a fair and reasonable manner.' This reflected an earlier minute of 1990 from the Joint Area Council looking at a range of arguments over alleged discrimination and disruption:

> Mr Kemmy stated that there was no point in going over the details of these grievances as . . . a new start would be made and that with good will the suggested local sub-committee would look into any allegations of discrimination . . . in the context of Mr Kemmy's suggestion it was agreed that all present should shake hands and hopefully a new start would be made.

Joe O'Brien of the Construction Industry Federation confirmed this to the author:

Jim Kemmy would make the case strongly for his members, an assertive negotiator, but Jim was very honourable. When you had an agreement with him, you knew it would stand and he would stick by it. There were some occasions when his own members went out of line and broke an agreement, but Jim was the first to pull them back when that happened. Jim stuck to the agreed procedures, there were no 'wild-cat' strikes with Jim.

As a further echo of this, Dan Miller reported to the author:

Jim worked as a trade union official on the Aughinisah Alumina building site in the early 1980s. There were some extreme left-wing union members on the Aughinish site, Jim felt they needed to be counter-balanced.

The shifting social context also had a substantial impact on Jim Kemmy's approach. Pat Reeves told the author:

The social gap between the building contractors and the tradesmen was not wide. Often, the contractors would have been tradesmen themselves, who started their own building businesses, but the social gap grew with the second generation – their children might have gone to bigger schools and had less connections with the employees. Also, small local builders in the 1960s began to be replaced by bigger national building companies and this made the employer/employee relationship more remote and more distant, more formal. All this affected Jim Kemmy.

The University of Limerick files are replete with copious correspondence from Kemmy lobbying for his members' interests, and frequently intervening to support individuals in personal difficulties. The list of issues was never-ending: personal references for jobs, advice with job seeking, assistance with applications for courses, securing apprenticeships for young entrants to the masons' trade, sorting out holiday pay entitlements, representations with employment appeals, helping workers cope with redundancy, highlighting the problem of accidents at work, promoting union membership, collection of union subscriptions, advice to members with income tax affairs, promoting access to welfare schemes such as sick pay, early retirement, medical cards and applications for death grants. Resolving problems with pensions was a frequent challenge. In several cases, Kemmy found that retiring union members did not have full entitlement to the pension scheme of the Construction Industry Federation. This was a mandatory scheme with contributions by employers and employees. A number of cases emerged of difficulties, caused either by lack of records by the employer or the employee. Support by Kemmy with tracking the details of contributions was critical for some people. In some cases, absence of payments by an employer, or liquidation of a building firm, presented special challenges and needs.

Jim Kemmy's style in helping people is illustrated by this comment: 'His filing cabinet was his inside pocket,' according to trade unionist Mike McNamara, 'stuffing notes of jobs-to-do for people in need of help of one sort or another.'

Pat Reeves told the author:

> If you hadn't trade unionists like Jim Kemmy, employers would walk all over you. Sometimes, you might find employers who did not make the pension contributions, and people only found out they were not covered for a pension after they retired, or worse, their wives found out after they had died. We did the best we could to avoid that kind of tragedy.

This concern for members' welfare extended especially to health and safety. According to Joe O'Brien of the Construction Industry Federation:

Jim was ahead of his time on health and safety matters
– he would get extremely annoyed if one of his members was being put in an unsafe or perilous situation on
a building site. This was in the 1980s, when health and
safety was not the big issue it is today, and the regulations[9] then were much less formal and defined.

Collective Approaches

Maintaining a unified approach among the different interests among the craft unions was a second set of challenges for
Kemmy. A major issue here for Jim Kemmy and the stonemasons was to confront the problem of 'lumping'. This was people working for lower than agreed wage rates and frequently
without social welfare benefits and tax contributions. Sick pay
and pension schemes were also ignored. 'Lumpers' worked
as independent sub-contractors outside recognised industry
schemes, and could cost the employer as much as 40 per cent
less than the conventional worker – a significant saving. The
campaign against this included court cases against the lumpers and employers. Also, building sites employing lumpers
were picketed by Kemmy's group.

According to Foncie McCoy, the 'lumping' problem faced
by Kemmy and his compatriots was built well into the system:

> Many masons would work the lump – this was money un-
> der the table. General workers would be working with ma-
> sons who might be working the lump, but getting no extra
> money and without security. The general worker worked
> on the building site alongside the mason, arranged the
> blocks and the mason would set the blocks up.

Pat Reeves reported that the 'lump' system was a big problem:

It was piece-rate, people would be paid per brick or per block. The trade unions did not want this as it undermined their agreements with the employers, but it was done on the quiet. But with the lump system social welfare cards were not being stamped, there were no pension contributions, so there was obviously havoc when people lost their job or retired. Lumping created a big headache for Jim Kemmy. The unions would police Limerick City for non-members. We fought for pay and conditions and we wanted to hold on to what we had achieved. But in some cases, Kemmy had to close his eyes to lumping practices – guys were making a lot of money, working outside the agreed rates of pay, and Jim would not be able to keep track of it. Lumping brought very poor workmanship, poor safety standards – money changes people, a big problem for Jim Kemmy, he dealt with it as best as he could. You had to watch out for the 'lump', the big problem was that people had nothing when work ran out.

There was controversy between the branches of the stonemasons union over allowing these 'sub-contractors' into the union. In 1984, representatives of the Kerry branch argued that it had been agreed to allow sub-contractors providing they did not employ members. But Jim Kemmy disagreed with this saying that he would not tolerate sub-contractors. In 1985, lumping in Clare was an issue, with people arguing that even the branch secretary of the union was working as a sub-contractor. The branch secretary was asked to step down. Books and receipts had been requested from the secretary. Kemmy said that the problem in Clare was particularly delicate – there were serious problems in relation to the use of lumpers and it appeared that the practice had been condoned in Clare for some time. Kemmy said it was important to maintain an organisation in the Clare area, but if members of the Clare branch were not prepared to work within the current structures of the union, then the branch would have to be dissolved and the transfer to neighbouring branches of those members who conformed. In the same year, there was further conflict between the Limerick and Kerry branches over differences in approaches to lumping: Limerick argued that Kerry were permitting lumping but Kerry denied this, with Jim Kemmy intervening on several occasions.

These inter-county differences were not unusual among the stonemasons, and spread to other issues. Joe O'Brien of the Construction Industry Federation told the author:

> There was frequently tension between the brick-layers in Limerick and those in Clare and Kerry. This was all about the local craft unions protecting their territory against those in neighbouring counties. Jim would have been part of this situation, and he would have been in a position of influence and would not necessarily accept a craftsman from another county. This 'blocking' of craftsmen from outside Limerick definitely caused problems for employers on some occasions, but it was part and parcel of the make-up of the building industry at the time.

But there were still other controversies among the stonemasons. In 1980, the stonemasons union was forced to establish an emergency sub-committee to examine alleged irregularities within the union. Disputes centred around conduct of certain members in Dublin. Charges included violent and abusive language, neglect of member complaints, assaults and selective promotion of the interests of some members. Altercations took place outside the union headquarters in Dublin, the conduct of the general president of the union being heavily criticised. Jim Kemmy was a member of the sub-committee, reporting that rival groups in Dublin were in contention for influence within the union. The sub-committee noted a conflict of evidence between the different reports, and that there was not much point in making 'recommendations' that might not be implemented. The sub-committee called on both sides to work together and to reconcile their differences.

Kemmy was also active in the work of the Limerick Building Trades Group, a cooperation between plasterers, electricians, bricklayers (i.e. stonemasons), plumbers and carpenters in the local building industry. The work of the group was vital in creating a common purpose among the different union interests, with Kemmy acting as secretary for several years. Initially established in 1957, the Building Trades Group brought together the major trades in the building industry. The initial impetus for the Building Trades Group grew from the common problem of non-craft labour doing craft work, and was set out in the first minutes: 'A laxity has crept in among the building trades that had developed in the boom years when outside contractors were allowed carry on as they liked.' Kemmy represented the stonemasons in the Building Trades Group as early as 1961, soon after his return from London, reflecting his early passion for the trade union movement. Minutes of meetings at that time illustrated his active role, noting his concern that 'three masons, union members, had been dismissed by their employer, and he was concerned about the credentials of two remaining masons'. Other topics raised by Kemmy over the years included safety issues, agreements with the construction industry, conflict with employers and other topics. Kemmy threw himself into the fray of the Building Trades Group, the group closely matching his growing awareness about worker unity and collective action, becoming secretary eventually.

Foncie McCoy, secretary of the Painters Society, told the author:

> I was the youngest member of the Building Trades Group when Jim Kemmy arrived. It was in 1961. The Group had

been established before, the Masons had pulled out, there was a lot of internal dissent at the time. There were five craft unions involved: carpenters, painters, masons, plumbers and plasterers. Jim Kemmy was very dour when he came to his first meeting, but I was delighted to see a young person like myself, and he was a real addition to the Building Trades Group.

According to Pat Reeves:

The Building Trades Group helped the relationship between the contractors and the unions – the contractors accepted the unions as a result. But you only brought things into the Building Trades Group if you had a big problem, you tried to sort things out within your own local area first. The relationships within the Building Trades Group were very good, there were differences in the way different unions approached things, but common sense ruled eventually – Jim Kemmy was very active in the Group and kept a firm grip on it.

But the Building Trades Group was fraught with difficulties in bringing together such fragmented participants, and there was suspicion among many of the constituent interests. As secretary of the group, Jim Kemmy had to work hard to maintain unity and overcome divisions or tensions among the members. For example, in 1966, a letter from the Union of Construction, Allied Trades and Technicians declared: 'The union which I represent are quite capable of looking after the interests of the union without the interference of any other members of the group in our affairs.' In 1970, a letter from the Plasterers Society insisted on unanimity on any decisions, and refused to accept majority voting: 'Members of the plasterers society will take part in any action by the Limerick Building Trades, provided it is decided unanimously by the Group.'

Later, in 1984, members of the Plasterers Society objected to 'interference' in their affairs by the Building Trades Group.

Foncie McCoy told the author:

> You could see some tension in the Building Trades Group. People would say, 'why are you going to all those meetings, the other unions will just hold us up,' so the work of Kemmy in keeping it together was very important.

In spite of these reservations, the Building Trades Group was successful in mobilising the different union interests in the local building industry. Issues confronted over the years included legal entitlements, travelling time, disturbance money, non-trade union members employed in the building industry, employment practices, annual leave entitlements, social employment schemes, new housing grants, parity of building workers with other workers, use of non-union subcontractors and other concerns. The key role for the Building Trades Group was to interact with the employers' Construction Industry Federation through the Area Joint Council of the Building Industry.

Foncie McCoy explained:

> As secretary of the Building Trades Group, Jim Kemmy was very active in this. You could bring up any problem relevant to the building industry, like an individual pension situation, special grants or anything.

Apart from the Building Trades Group, a second collective association where Kemmy was active was the Limerick Trades Council, acting as chairman and spokesman from the mid-1960s to 1975. This was an umbrella group for the trades, not only the building trades (carpenters, brick layers, plumbers), but also a wider set of trades such as electricians, fitters and toolmakers, many involved in the manufacturing sector. This Council monitored local happenings and watched working conditions, lobbying for improvements in terms of employment for their members. Maintaining a unified approach was important, and the Trades Council had to work hard to encourage members to go through official channels in the case of industrial disputes. For example, during the construction of the giant Ferenka factory in the 1970s, several unofficial disputes broke out among the trades, demanding strong responses from the Trades Council. 'There were all shades of opinions in the Trades Council, so it was hard work for Jim to secure a collective approach,' reported Joe Kemmy.

Joe Wallace of the University of Limerick explained:

> I met Jim first in the late 1970s at a meeting of the Limerick Trades Council where he was a delegate. In 1978 I had been employed by the then National Institute for Higher Education (now the University of Limerick) to undertake a survey of industrial relations in Limerick city and environs. This was done in the wake of the 1977 Ferenka dispute and naturally there were tensions and raw nerves as a result of the closure of that plant on foot of an inter-union dispute. Limerick was being portrayed in the media as having special industrial relations problems and we set out to document the actual state of play and to make comparisons with other large urban centers in Ireland.
>
> As part of the study it was decided to conduct a survey of personnel managers and shop stewards in Limerick city and environs and we needed the support of the trade unions in undertaking the shop steward part of the survey. Jim was particularly helpful in getting the Trades Council to endorse the survey. I made a presentation of our proposed research to a meeting of the Council. There was natural concern at our proposal given the raw nerves. Jim was silent during most of the discussion, then, about two-thirds of the way through the meeting, he made an emphatic statement that the study should be supported

and if the trade unions deserved criticism then so be it. He added that we should not be afraid of being critical if that was deserved and that unions should be open to this. With that, the other delegates seemed to relax and we quickly got overwhelming support for the study. This was an example to me of the charisma he had and the moral 'suasion' he could evoke. It was also to me an early indication of his distinctive style of being very emphatic and taking clear position on issues.

Joe Wallace concluded:

It is important to recognise that the Limerick Trades Council had relevance outside the trade union movement at that time as it was the launching pad for several politicians, Jim Kemmy included. While Jim was a skilled craft worker he identified with the broader labour movement and this enabled him to build a wide base of support in working class areas. It is also notable that in the 1960s and 1970s he was very much to the left of trade union politics in Limerick as he adopted strong emphatic, socialist positions and views. Both his supporters and opponents knew where they stood with him.

Apprenticeship System

A third focus of Kemmy and his colleagues in the union was the apprenticeship system, where Kemmy was active in promoting reform. In those days, the craft unions controlled the apprenticeship system and dictated entry. In the early years of his involvement with the craft unions, he was struck by how much the stonemasons operated as a 'closed shop', restricting entry to only the sons and relatives of members. Kemmy worked actively to create a more open entry system to the stonemasons' craft, and in promoting improvements to the apprenticeship system.

Kemmy strived to make the stonemasons a more open union, seeing it almost as a 'secret society', restricted to sons of stonemasons, and only occasionally open to other family members, such as nephews. Jim Kemmy worked intensively to open the stonemasons to the wider society. Some resisted the opening up of the stonemasons, but this coincided with a time of economic boom and opportunity. Kemmy had to do this very carefully, without making it a big issue. 'Jim Kemmy had no time for elitism of stonemasons; he wanted an open and wider trade union system,' reported Joe Kemmy.

The context in which Kemmy had to work was described to the author by Foncie McCoy:

> The masons were like gods, they were a self-preservation society. All the trades at the time were father-to-son, even a stepson would not get into a trade. There were some special rules, such as the plasterers where the son of an eldest sister might get in. Also, there were limitations on outsiders. If a person came from the country without full union membership, he might be called a 'pressure of work man', taken on only when the pressure of work demanded it, then let go in favour of a craftsman.

Mike McNamara, secretary of the Building and Allied Trades Union (BATU), told the author how he first met Kemmy in the 1980s: 'My first memory of himself was as a young man shaking Kemmy's massive hand.' McNamara wanted to enter the masons trade: 'Jim Kemmy gave me a reassuring pat on the back to assure me that everything would be all right, but he was so strong it almost drove me down the stairs!'

Up to the 1960s, the 'indenture' system prevailed in the masons trade – apprentices were indentured to a master craftsman, often their father, with indentures being authorised by the public authorities. As branch secretary, Jim Kemmy had to approve each indenture. The system was very hierarchical, with master craftsmen being addressed by the apprentice as 'sir', reported Mike McNamara.

Dan Miller told the author:

> Jim was secretary of the stonemasons in Limerick for 39 years; he was managing a lot of things over that time. Jim was active in the craft guild. Tradesmen in the 1960s had an elitist view of themselves, how you served your time, who you where, where you were from. Kemmy had none of that, he was no elitist, he saw the guild as a vehicle through which people could improve themselves – mobility for people, not locked into father-to-son relationships, he was a anxious to facilitate young people. Many craft unions restricted entry to the sons of craft workers. People saw it as step up to be a craftsman, but Jim wanted to create opportunities for young people to participate in the crafts. Kemmy saw the whole line of young people coming up through the trade. He facilitated a lot of young people to become craftsmen, something the purists in the guild objected to vehemently.

Pat Reeves reported: 'The local trades were all family – you couldn't get into a craft union unless you were related.'

With the establishment of AnCo (An Comhairle Oiliúna – the training council) in 1967, the indenture system gave way to time-served apprenticeships, for five years, in contrast to the old seven-year indenture, including attendance at school for one day per week, subsequently shortened to four year apprenticeships, with nine months in school off the job. Kemmy was instrumental in the development of the new system. People on the branch committee became teachers. The apprenticeship system then included two ten-week block-release courses, with junior trade exams and senior trade exams. The shift in the apprenticeships to open access came under AnCo, new apprentices were not constrained by not being related to masons, and the restriction of entry to the mason trade to family members of existing craftsmen was lifted. Many masons were understandably reluctant and even opposed to this change, but Jim Kemmy championed it enthusiastically. Mike McNamara reported: 'He was way ahead of his time, saw the need to open up the trade, could see that the future of the trade was dependent on being opened up to new entrants.'

Foncie McCoy explained to the author how Kemmy would have been affected by those changes:

> In the one-to-four rule you had to have four men on a job before you could take on an apprentice; the employers wanted to take on more young people – the boys were cheaper. AnCo wanted to remove the limit, build up the workforce – you had people in trades just because their father was there, round pegs in square holes.

Joe Kemmy said:

> Kemmy had to lobby builders to take on apprentices. While there was this unwritten rule that for every four tradesmen there would be one apprentice, the builders did not want to actually train apprentices, so Jim had to lobby hard.

In the late 1980s, the 'time served' apprenticeship was replaced by a 'standards-based' apprenticeship, with seven phases: on the job, FÁS centre (successor to AnCo), on the job, Limerick Institute of Technology, on the job, Limerick Institute of Technology, on the job. Apprenticeships could be four to five years, depending on exam success, or the willingness of the employer to release apprentices to schools. Kemmy actively encouraged such new reforms. He saw them as strengthening and developing the masons' craft, but also encouraged flexibility and adapting to the needs of individual circumstances. 'People had to have the Group Certificate to get into apprenticeship, but Jim helped to arrange special cases to get apprenticeship without the Group Certificate,' said Joe Kemmy.

In an undated memo, Kemmy wrote about his views on necessary reforms:

> Craft unions have always been intimately concerned with training and recruitment of apprentices. The level of attainment of Irish apprentices in international competitions is evidence of this. There is a crucial need for off-the-job training for apprentices. But this will give the apprentices only the basic skills and the remaining period of the apprenticeship should be under the supervision of a competent craftsman.
>
> The employer should provide proper job rotation. However, there is a tendency for employers to use apprentices for menial jobs. Assessment of apprentices should not be by employers alone: supervisory tradesmen should also be involved.
>
> Apprentices should be primarily trained to meet their needs as craftsmen, and secondly, though an intricate part of this, to meet the ends of the industry in which they work. During training, account should be taken of the possible future needs of craftsmen and of industry, and the possibility that craftsmen might be forced to work in other countries.
>
> Length of apprenticeship should be related to the time necessary to acquire the skills, experience and familiarity with the industry that is essential for the craftsman. Block release courses are invaluable.

In 1983, Kemmy disputed allegations that there were not enough places of employment for AnCo trainees in the building industry. An argument had been made by union members that AnCo was recruiting too many trainees in the building industry. Kemmy argued that employment was satisfactory for trainees under the umbrella of the Bricklayers and Stonemasons Union. 'We try to find places for them and we are committed to their cause,' he reported. Although Jim Kemmy also acknowledged that the building industry was going through a rough period at the time, AnCo fulfilled a worthwhile role and had the full support of the Bricklayers and Stonemasons Union. But union opponents argued that Kemmy, by that particular time, did not work in the building industry any more and that 'he was out of touch with real happenings'.[10]

Dan Miller told the author:

> Technology changes affected the guild. The masons adopted piece-work before other guilds, with payment by output. Some of the earliest productivity agreements were to stonemasons, with 'de-skilling', the role of stonemason began to be superseded by brick-layers and later by block-layers. This process had to be managed by the union, particularly the need to keep standards up and workmanship up. In boom years, standards dropped with output taking precedence over everything else. Jim Kemmy saw the need to distinguish between putting bricks on bricks and the craft of the stonemasons – he was anxious to keep the craft of stonemasons alive.

Joe O'Brien of the Construction Industry Federation commented:

> Jim was very conscious of the needs of young apprentices. They were starting out on their careers in the building industry so they would be obviously vulnerable. He bent over backwards to help apprentices who might have been made redundant by, say, a building contractor going out of business. In those cases, Jim Kemmy would strive hard to find an alternative employer to take them on. This was very important as otherwise the apprentice concerned

would find his apprenticeship interrupted, with very damaging consequences for his career. At Jim's instigation, we set up a special committee involving AnCO (the then industrial training authority), Construction Industry Federation and the Building Trades Group. Here we pooled our resources to find alternative employers for apprentices who became redundant. This turned out to be very successful in arranging placements – it was an innovative first by Limerick and, as a result, it was copied and emulated around the country.

Joe O'Brien concluded:

Jim Kemmy was like a one-man employment agency – he would actively find jobs for apprentices, and also for fully qualified brick-layers. If he sent you somebody, you knew they would be all right, and Jim would have checked them out. If there was a problem afterwards, Jim would always follow up and try to resolve things, so you learnt to have good trust in him.

The Mechanics' Institute

Jim Kemmy based himself in the 'Mechanics' Institute[11] in Hartstonge Street in Limerick, a particular entity that formed a central part of his life. These Institutes were developed in the nineteenth century in Britain in response to the growing working class of the industrial revolution, with the aim to instruct the 'artisans' or mechanics in the scientific principles underlying their trade. Established in the early 1800s, the Mechanics' Institute in Limerick aimed for an educated workforce of skilled labour, providing the base for the Limerick Trades Council, the consortium of skilled trade unions in the Limerick area.

The late Jim Kemmy's association with the Limerick Mechanics' Institute is well known. Kemmy was working in Shannon at the time and at the invitation of Charlie O'Flynn (president of the stonemasons) started to attend meetings in the Mechanics' Institute as a delegate member of the masons in 1961. Jim Kemmy became president of the Mechanics' Institute in 1976, until his death in 1997, making a generous and valuable contribution to the Institute. Kemmy always encouraged the delegate board in the Mechanics' Institute to involve itself in the wider community and not to concentrate solely on the union or craft issues. Jim Kemmy loved the Mechanics' Institute and spent a lot of time in it. He returned to it in triumph on many occasions, flushed with political victory. He also returned disappointed and dejected on a cold day in November 1982 having lost his Dáil seat. On his election to the Dáil in 1981, the minutes of the delegate board of the Mechanics' Institute noted: 'Jim Kemmy was very conscious of the support given him by the Delegate Board, he was very proud of the Mechanics' Institute, his success had been a team effort. He recalled he had been introduced to trade unions in the Mechanics' Institute and that one of the first union meetings he had attended had been at the Delegate Board. He thanked the Board for allowing him the use of a room during his campaign.'[12]

But there was dissension as well. Later, in 1984, correspondence[13] from J. Costelloe angrily argued that Kemmy and his party, the DSP, were being given, free of rent, the advantage of offices and political clinics at the Institute. This represented sponsorship of a political party and was unconstitutional under the Institute's constitution:

It can be said that never in the history of the Mechanics Institute have so many abuses been carried out by any one individual. As far as I am concerned Kemmy and his party are no more than squatters in the Mechanics Institute.

Thus Kemmy's unlimited capacity for controversy inevitably followed him into the Mechanics' Institute!

Support given by the Mechanics' Institute to the union movement in Limerick included training of trade union officials, support to shop stewards, information point on trade union topics, advice centre and health screening. The social scene surrounding the Mechanics' Institute was of significant importance to Limerick. The Institute had a strong record in making available its resources for cultural, social and sporting activities. The long single-storey building in Hartstonge Street was used as an assembly hall, and also provided facilities for concerts, dances, card drives and bingo. Plays and dramas featured as well in the Mechanics' Institute.

Kemmy's work with the Mechanics' Institute is well illustrated by an incident recounted by Mike McNamara:

Jim Kemmy made the Mechanics' Institute available to all sort of groups to hold meetings. Over the years, some people took advantage of his hospitality and would often just turn up and ask the caretaker for a room, the caretaker would oblige and re-arrange the meeting rooms without any discussion with the unions. On one particular occasion a worker turned up to join the engineering trade union. He went into the meeting room as directed in the correspondence he had received, took a seat in the body of the room as there were a few people sitting around the big table at the top. Within minutes a very heated exchange took place between the men at the top table, then they began pushing and shoving and a row erupted, with violent blows being exchanged. The newcomer ran out in terror for help, bumping into 'Big Jim' in the corridor. Jim dashed into the room to break up the commotion, only to discover that the Quarry Players (a local drama group) had shown up un-announced to rehearse an up-coming play!

Kemmy shared his ideas and thoughts with many through the Mechanics' Institute. Foncie McCoy told the author:

> We would work late every Friday at the Mechanics' Institute. Each of the unions had an office, carpenters, electricians, painters, meeting trade union members, collecting dues, responding to problems. Walking home with Jim every Friday evening, we would talk about everything. Once in the early 1960s, on the election of Donagh O'Malley (popular Fianna Fáil minister from Limerick), Jim told me then he was even thinking of joining the Fianna Fáil party! We would talk about what was happening in government, how to improve conditions, get more money, often discuss how it would be better to look for improved conditions, rather than money – money can get devalued by inflation, or reduced, but conditions are something you always had . . . so it was brain-storming all the time.

Kemmy the Trade Unionist

Jim Kemmy brought his stonemason background into the mainstream of his political life. For example, opening a geology conference in 1988 in his role as a TD, he said:

> I believe that at a time when concrete, steel, glass and other such materials predominate, stone still has an important role to play in modern building. But to survive and expand that role, we must make stone relevant and attractive . . . we must cut out our own work in every sense of the word.[14]

On a wider set of issues, Kemmy's negotiation skills were highlighted in remarks to a University of Limerick summer school: 'You have to settle for the best you can in this free trade and unregulated world we live in and there is no point in saying the management is wrong, or should be turfed out, if you have no job at the end of the day.'[15]

Kemmy's role as a trade unionist also influenced his work as a representative in the City Council. At one time, there was a dispute in the City Council cleansing department. As secretary of the Building Trades Group, Kemmy said that he was anxious that the dispute should not spread.[16] Also, at a City Council meeting, an appeal for reconciliation between unions was made by Jim Kemmy:

> At a time of so much inter-union strife, perhaps a lesson can be learnt from the manner in which building unions work together and cooperate, not only at the a national level but also at local level. In the present Ferenka dispute – the most difficult and bitter in Limerick's industrial relations history – something has to be learnt from the manner in which building unions work together. You need a similar attitude and compromise among workers working together in the same industry.[17]

Foncie McCoy told the author:

Jim Kemmy worked in Limerick City Council as a mason, but he wasn't really a firebrand all the time there – the Council would have one person detailed to talk to the unions. The general workers (roadsweepers, cleansing department) were very fiery, they would strike at the drop of a hat. Jim would lead deputations to the council officials. There were a lot of demarcation disputes. He wouldn't let them leave a stone on a block. Some general operatives might start laying blocks, but that would be a matter from the masons, general operative would set up the blocks, but the mason would put them in position. Sometimes, if a general operative put the blocks in position, there would be a dispute. As secretary of the Building Trades Group, Kemmy was active in the City Council. The cleansing people were very awkward. Jim did not like

being with them. They had their own set ways, no give
and take. Kemmy needed their votes at election, so he
had to be careful – they would never compromise, they
knew they were essential.

As Chairman of the National Monuments Advisory Committee of Limerick City Council, Kemmy said that city trea-
sures were being lost due to council carelessness. Precious
items were either decaying or mislaid in careless storage.
Kemmy encouraged the Limerick Trades Council to support a
proposal by Thomond Archaeological Society to improve museum facilities.[18] Dan Miller told the author: 'Jim understood
the importance of the masons' skills in his local government
work, his involvement in conservation, like historic sites and
buildings in Limerick would have been spurred by his mason's
insights.'

As Mayor of Limerick in the 1990s, Kemmy worked behind
the scenes in discussions with management and unions in an
effort to bring about a successful outcome on bin strike settlement talks.[19]

Margaret O'Donoghue commented: 'Jim was always coming and going between his union work and the City Council,
often rushing in from the building sites, frantically rubbing
the mud off his shoes, to dash down town to a council meeting!'

Commenting on Kemmy's role as a trade unionist, his
brother Joe Kemmy told the author that Jim Kemmy had a
good relationship with most employers, with only two strikes
in 20 years by the stonemasons. Kemmy was an effective negotiator and did deals with the builders – many builders wanted
to solve problems to secure good industrial relations on their
sites. One strike was against Portland Estates, seeking trade
union recognition for a stonemason. Following the stoppage,
pickets were placed on the building site. The employer gave

way and recognised the union. Rates of pay rose for the masons as a result. The second strike was against the post office where, in the construction of man-holes, they had used contractors without recognised stonemasons. The post office HQ in Limerick was picketed – at one stage scuffles broke out and gardaí were called. The post office authorities settled after one week of stoppage. Other disputes were sorted without strikes. These were almost always about pay and conditions. The masons had no strike in Ferenka (which closed in Limerick in 1977, with 1,700 job losses, following a lengthy and bitter industrial dispute), although there were continuous strikes among other trade unions. Masons had no grievance with Ferenka.

'Jim Kemmy was good at solving problems,' reported Joe Kemmy:

> Bricklayers often were paid more than other trades, like carpenters and plasterers. Everyone had a flat rate of pay and the builders would pay extra with negotiation. Jim was very good at negotiating extra rates. The builders wanted trouble-free sites and were agreeable to settle for better terms and conditions.

In later years, the pressures arising from the multiplicity of large numbers of small unions leading to fragmentation, weakened representation and rising costs attracted increasing attention and concern. Policy shifted to strengthening the union system through rationalisation, amalgamations and mergers. Jim Kemmy was active in this movement for reform, conscious of the need to amalgamate unions, and fully aware of the impending demise of the small craft unions. By 1977, there was active discussion between the unions about amalgamation, with Kemmy and the masons lobbying strongly for unity among the construction trades. Inevitably, small unions had very limited funds, with weak ability to support any kind of strike-pay in the event of an industrial dispute. Simply to survive, unions had to get bigger. The amalgamation in 1988 was between three unions: stonecutters, masons and wood machinists (carpenter and joinery tradesmen) to form the Building and Allied Trades' Union (BATU), with Kemmy acting as local secretary to the new union.

Throughout his union activities, Kemmy's direct and forceful style matured and developed over the years, and was very much a hallmark of his approach. But Jim Kemmy was certainly not one given over to tolerance. In one case, according to Mike McNamara, a union member was lobbying Kemmy for help with employment. The particular member was a religious fundamentalist, sort of a born-again Christian, full of strict and devout religion in his everyday conversation. In exasperation, the atheist Jim Kemmy retorted: 'You tell us the Lord shall provide, and you're looking at me to get you a job!' Kemmy's low tolerance in many aspects was further echoed by Dan Miller:

> During the 1960s, in relation to alcohol, Jim was a staunch temperance enthusiast, although this changed in later life. He had a very negative attitude to drink. At one stage he had a senior figure of the local trade union movement who was partial to drink, getting drunk at some official function. Jim rounded on him: 'you're a disgrace to the trade union movement.' He had a big issue with people letting down the trade unions by drink.

Pat Reeves told the author:

> Jim Kemmy was radical, left wing, socialist. When he joined first in the trade union movement, he was quiet, finding his feet, but then came the fire and brimstone; he didn't necessarily cause havoc, but he certainly created difficulties for employers. The Building Trades Group had to pull Jim Kemmy back a few times, he thought he was

'God' on some occasions, he needed to be reined back, but you would never rein back Jim in front of employers, this all happened behind the scenes. However, even though he was a firebrand, there were very few incidents where Jim Kemmy caused a strike.

Pat Reeves concluded:

Jim Kemmy made a real force of the stonemasons, he got them together, and he also helped mobilise the Building Trades Group as a force to be recognised. Kemmy would never go into deals behind closed doors, he did not like negotiating in private or in secrecy.

Foncie McCoy explained:

Jim Kemmy was a very dominant personality. Jim would push very hard to get something done. It did not help to go against him. At one meeting, the chair of the masons voted against the wishes of Jim at a Building Trades Group meeting, to be confronted angrily afterwards by Kemmy: 'take that chain of office off your unworthy neck'. Jim was a firebrand in his early days, but became more mellow in later years. Jim was quick to go for disputes in his early days. Once, an official of the union said, 'Kemmy is too fiery, he doesn't see the full picture', but he became easier in his negotiation style in later years. Jim softened over the years, lost a lot of the fire, but maybe he learnt and just got more clever.

Joe O'Brien of the Construction Industry Federation reported:

I would not paint him as a 'saint', of course, he defended his members' interests very strongly, and that inevitably led to conflict with the employers in some instances, and things could be very difficult then. But there was no agenda about Jim Kemmy, he was a good straight-forward, honest fellow. You knew where you stood with him, and how far you could push him; there were no hidden issues, he wanted to protect his members, he had no personal hostility to employers, but just his desire to get the best deal for his people. That was the beauty of dealing with Jim, what you saw was what you got – if he had a problem, you would know all about it. We knew where he was coming from, and we could deal with that.

This was reflected in comments by Dan Miller to the author:

Jim Kemmy was pragmatic, a pragmatic trade unionist, a pragmatic socialist, he judged things strategically. Say, managing a group of construction workers, he would be the intellectual head, he would try his best to bring people around to a consensus point of view, that was where his pragmatism came in. Kemmy would never have won a popularity contest, but he knew he had to win respect, 'people do not have to like you to respect you', he often said.

This brusqueness was confirmed by Anna-Maria Hajba:

Jim Kemmy was very blunt, said it as he saw it. In fact, he seemed to have been blunt to the point of rudeness, very forceful, big man, strong physical presence, single motivation. Made of stone in some ways, he couldn't have been anything else, when you have a block of stone you carve out of it what you want, he did that mentally, the same determination, the same commitment to all his work. There were no secrets about Jim Kemmy, everything was all out in the open, you can see that in the single mindedness.

Jim Kemmy – Trade Unionist

The chart below illustrates the system of building trade unions in Limerick during Jim Kemmy's time.

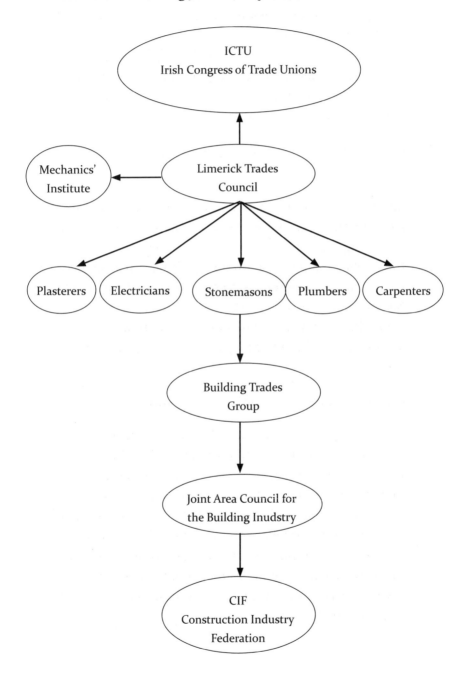

Endnotes

1. Sources for this section are the Kemmy Collection in the University of Limerick, unless stated otherwise.

2. *Limerick Leader*, 9 March 1963.

3. *Industrial Relations in Ireland* (third edition) by Joseph Wallace, Patrick Gunnigle and Gerard McMahon (Gill and Macmillan, 2004).

4. Union of Soviet Socialist Republics.

5. Luke Verling, 1999.

6. *History of the Ancient Guild of Incorporated Brick and Stonelayers Society, 1670-1970: A short history* by Frank O'Connor, General Secretary , 1971 (Kemmy Collection, UL).

7. Address by Jim Kemmy to the Tuairim meeting, Savoy Cinema, Limerick, 1969 (Kemmy Collection, UL).

8. Luke Verling, 1999.

9. It was not until the 1989 Health and Safety Act that employers were specifically required to ensure the health, safety and welfare of their employees.

10. *Limerick Leader*, 14 November 1983.

11. Correspondents vary in their punctuation of the title: Mechanics Institute, Mechanic's Institute and Mechanics' Institute. Kemmy, reflecting his rigorous discipline and attention to detail, always used the third and correct version, with the apostrophe outside the 's' (the possessive plural).

12. 'An Analysis of the Mechanics' Institute' by Sarah Duff (unpublished student project, University of Limerick, 2003).

13. Kemmy Collection, UL.

14. Opening Address by Jim Kemmy, TD, to the Irish Geology Week Conference, Athlone, 1988.

15. *Limerick Leader*, 23 July 1994.

16. *Limerick Leader*, 13 September 1976.

17. *Limerick Leader*, 7 November 1977.

18. *Limerick Leader*, 16 December 1978.

19. *Limerick Leader*, 8 September 1995.

8

Final Days

The final days for Jim Kemmy have been recounted by Ray Kavanagh. Under the heading 'farewell sweet prince', Kavanagh explains in his book, how, on 24 June 1997, Jim Kemmy's secretary Margaret O'Donoghue telephoned him and, in an unusually subdued tone, said that Jim Kemmy wanted to talk to him.

> I wanted to tell you something, Ray. I was not feeling too well during the campaign and I thought I'd broken a rib. It has been now confirmed that I have multiple myloma, which is bone marrow cancer, and it is irreversible.

Almost as if he was describing a new coat he said, 'I'll be happy if I get two years out of it. I want you to keep it quiet for a while.' Jim Kemmy attended his last meeting of the Parliamentary Labour Party on 26 June some days later and contributed to the proceedings.

Patsy Harold told the author that, the day Jim Kemmy received the bad news about his fatal illness, he still went to a trade union meeting that evening, and continued to work up to his dying breath. Jim Kemmy had lung problems associated with asbestos from working in the building industry during the

1960s, and this probably contributed to his illness. 'Jim had felt unwell during the election, he was coughing a lot and he had a pain and thought it was some muscle pulled by bending down to put election leaflets into letterboxes, but, no, it was much worse.' Patsy also felt that at the time she was concentrating on a course in Mary Immaculate College and 'maybe I didn't notice enough'. According to Seamus Harrold, 'In the 1960s, Jim had been lining the chimneys in the Cement factory in Mungret, near Limerick, and came into a lot of contact with asbestos.'

In the months remaining, Kemmy continued with his work. His last recorded speech was in July 1997 on the centenary of the birth of Kate O'Brien, the Irish novelist:

> It was in her exploration of the role of women in society that Kate O'Brien achieved her greatest breakthrough as a writer. She wrote about the unnatural sterility and cruel idleness of mind and body of the middle class women of Limerick. She laid bare the passion, tension and conflict of their inner lives. She revealed their silent suffering and suppressed cries.[1]

This was vintage Kemmy, combining so many of his themes: the socialist jibe at the class system, the liberating power of literature, the growth in freedom for women.

On 11 August, Ray Kavanagh met Jim Kemmy off the train at Heuston station in Dublin and brought him to the hospital. Kavanagh said it was heartbreaking to leave him there, far from home that night, but never once did he complain. Patsy Harrold, his friend, was with him and she was a rock of strength. They were both far stronger than Kavanagh thought he would be in a similar situation.

Around his bedside now assembled some of the intellectual and political figures of Ireland, and well as his family and friends. His humour never gave up and he was fascinated by his treatment. 'This chemotherapy is very interesting,' he told Kavanagh, 'the only problem is that I'm part of the experiment.' He went through the proofs of his last book, the *Limerick Compendium*. Mary Robinson was an early visitor, as was Bertie Ahearn, John Bruton and other members of the Oireachtas, as well as people from the media, cultural and political worlds, according to Ray Kavanagh.

Dick Spring was in America but on his return he went to visit Jim Kemmy. There was to be no deathbed reconciliation. Kemmy did not share the gentle hypocrisy of the Irish who generally make up with their enemies on their deathbeds, wrote Kavanagh. He was too honest in the bluntest sort of way. There was something fierce, something almost Old Testament in his truth that was not softened even by approaching death. Dick Spring told the author:

> I went to see Jim in the hospital. 'Things must be bad when you are coming to see me,' was the response I got from Jim – he knew his race was run.

Fergus Finlay telephoned Kemmy. Kavanagh was glad it was only that, a face-to-face showdown would have done neither of them any good. Fergus Finlay, of course, received the same treatment as Dick Spring, reported Kavanagh.

Jim Kemmy was gentle to the end, reported Niall Greene:

> He was in a lot of distress. Once, when I brought him a book, a bit of a tome – a history of socialism – he apologised that he was not really strong enough to read it.

Manus O'Riordan had a similar story:

> When Jim was in St James Hospital, I called in regularly. Jim was in great agony; bone cancer is a terrible thing. I would watch him in excruciating pain, it was measure of the man that he would be still thinking of other people but say, 'I'm sorry I'm not much company', but he would be talking about things he was reading up to the very end.

Jim Kemmy died on 25 September. Niall Greene told the author:

> It was tragic Jim died so young at 61, he deserved another term in the Dáil, maybe retire after that and spend happy retirement years researching and writing history. It was what should have happened, but that was not to be.

At the funeral,[2] men and women wept during a ceremony deliberately devoid of the pomposity which Kemmy detested – 10,000 were reported to have filed past his coffin. There had been no valedictory procession along the main thoroughfares of Limerick. Instead, the cortege took the shortest route from the funeral parlour to the cemetery, a clearly secular event. This would have reflected Manus O'Riordan's view: 'People had great respect for Jim Kemmy, even the most virulent political opponents, from both the left and right, had respect for him.'

At the city fire station, the engines lined up to flash their red lights in honour of Jim Kemmy as the hearse passed by. The hearse stopped once – outside the Pike Inn – meeting place for Kemmy supporters and canvassers for many years. Along the route, people stopped working and came out to see the last journey of one of their city's most famous citizens, reported the media.

Chief mourners were his friend, Patsy Harrold, his brother and right-hand man in Limerick, Joe, his sisters Maureen McAteer and Joan Hartnett, his halfbrother, P.J. Pilkington, and family member, Mary Troy. The graveside ceremony was opened by the mayor, Frank Leddin, who recalled Jim Kemmy's championing of poor and unemployed people and his work as a local historian.

According to Ray Kavanagh: 'This was to be a Labour funeral, and nobody was to be left in any doubt. It was an entirely secular affair in line with Jim's atheism.'

Final Days

Dick Spring summed up Kemmy's style when he said:

> What you saw was what you got with Jim Kemmy. There were no airs and graces and he never forgot his roots in the city of Limerick. Jim's relationship with our party had its ups and downs. Jim would say it was a turbulent relationship on both sides.

Spring recalled Kemmy's 'detestation of extreme nationalism' and the 1990 merger of his Democratic Socialist Party, whose founder-chairman, Seamus Rhatigan, was among the mourners, with the Labour Party in 1990. Dick Spring told the author:

> I was deeply honoured to be asked by Joe Kemmy to speak at the funeral. It was different kind of funeral, secular and humanist, Jim was true to his beliefs to the very end.

Jim Kemmy's funeral ended, at his request, with the recorded voice of John Hanson singing 'Beautiful Dreamer' to the subdued and sombre mourners in Mount St Lawrence Cemetery in Limerick City. There was also a reading by actor Mike Finn of Dylan Thomas's 'Do Not Go Gentle into that Good Night', requested by Kemmy.

Gearóid Ó Tuathaigh, as a historian, was invited by the Kemmy family to give a special funeral oration. This had been particularly requested by Kemmy on his death-bed: 'Jim wanted to be remembered not only as a political person and a trade unionist, but also wanted to be seen as a local historian – that was very important to him,' Joe Kemmy reported.

In the funeral oration, Ó Tuathaigh said that Kemmy was within a particular radical, dissenting tradition of the broad labour movement of the nineteenth century. Frequently engaging in bruising controversy, his steady commitment to a socialist and libertarian view of human fulfilment and dignity never slackened or wavered throughout a political career that was never routine, never complacent, never opportunistic. He held his own views firmly and he expressed them clearly, not to say trenchantly. But it was neither necessary, nor was it always the case, that one had to agree with his views in order to recognise in him that stubborn refusal to defer to received wisdom, to the official rhetoric of 'authority', or to any dogma (whatever its ideological origins) which failed to take account of the frailty, the longings, the complexities and the contradictions of ordinary human beings, buffeted by history and circumstance, by their own hopes, fears and desires. Though utterly unsympathetic to cant or slack sentiment, Jim Kemmy was a labour romantic, feeling part of the romance of the historic project of working-class emancipation, with its strong nineteenth century idealistic strain, especially but not exclusively in Britain. It is the tradition of the Durham miners, of working men's reading societies and mechanics institutes, of the early leaders of the Irish trade union and labour movement. Kemmy aimed to rescue the story and struggles of the common people from the terrible condescension of posterity.

Gearóid Ó Tuathaigh concluded:

> When I spoke in my opening remarks of his full and fulfilling life being all of a piece, what I had in mind was the sense that in all the political ups and downs, the battles lost and battles won, what sustained Jim Kemmy throughout was probably a profound conviction that, whatever the immediate clamour, he could hear and was in step with the deep insistent rhythm of the march of the common man towards liberty, dignity and a place in the sun.

Endnotes

1. Kemmy Collection (UL).

2. *Irish Times*, 30 September 1997.

Index

divorce, 16–7, 24, 36–7, 60
Drake, Peter, 139

'Exiled Memory 57', 8

family planning, 17, 29, 31–2, 60,
94, 106–7
Family Planning Association, 32
Ferrar, John, 147
Fianna Fáil, 11, 38, 43, 50, 76, 78,
90, 103
Fine Gael, 38, 83, 92, 103
Finlay, Fergus, 79–81, 193
Fitzgerald, Ernest, 106
Fitzgerald, Garret, 35, 38, 42–3,
92
Fourth Siege of Limerick, The,
136
French, Percy, 147

Gabay, Zvi, 114
Gallagher, Michael, 20, 24, 41
Garda Representative Associa-
tion, 46–7
Garryowen, 3, 135
Garryowen Residents' Associa-
tion, 117
Grapes of Wrath, The, 11–12
Greene, Niall, 21–22, 24–25, 35,
41, 49, 63, 70, 84, 87, 107, 194
Gregory, Tony, 58, 66

Hajba, Anna-Maria, 7, 117, 146,
188
Halligan, Brendan, 16, 26, 51, 126
Hannon, Kevin, 129–30
Hannon, Noel, 107
Harrold, Patsy, 17, 19, 77, 97, 110,
191–2, 194
Harrold, Seamus, 18, 27, 34, 38,
49–50, 52, 64, 65, 104, 108, 116,
126, 129, 145, 192

Hartnett, Joan (née Kemmy), 5,
194
Haughey, Charles, 44, 58, 65
Health Act, 1947, 6
Help Foundation Trust, 115
Herrema, Dr. Tiede, 125
Higgins, Michael D., 113
Hogan, Michael, 139
Hunt Museum, 104, 111, 113

Irish Citizen Army, 13
Irish Communist Organisation,
20, 55
Irish Congress of Trade Unions,
31
Kavanagh, Ray, 48, 66, 68, 70–2,
76–7, 82, 83, 87, 94, 118, 191,
194
Keating, Justin, 21
Kemmy Business School, 113
Kemmy Collection, 7, 158
Kemmy, Elizabeth (née Pilkington), 2, 5
Kemmy, Jim
abortion and, 48–52
anti-nationalist views of, 11, 31,
73, 75, 92, 108, 133, 195
apprenticeship as stonemason,
7–8
childhood of, 3–6
Church–State separation and,
16, 20, 29, 31, 33, 90
death of father, 6–7
death of mother, 17
divorce laws and, 36–37
Europe and, 73, 89
family planning and, 31–32
life in London, 9–13
Northern Ireland and, 25–26,
29–31, 36, 87, 108
religious views of, 16, 102

Ó Tuathaigh, Gearóid, 195–6
Old Limerick Journal, 102,
    127–30, 139, 144–6
Old Limerick Society, 127

Pilkington, P.J., 5, 194
Prendergast, Frank, 25, 35, 48,
    50, 69, 125
Pro-Life Amendment Cam-
    paign, 48
Progressive Democrats, 65, 76,
    83, 110
Provisional IRA, 31, 87

Questions and Answers, 47
Quinn, Ruairi, 86

*Ragged Trousered Philanthro-
    pists, The*, 12
Reeves, Pat, 2, 6, 7, 99, 156,
    164–5, 167, 170, 175, 186–7
Reynolds, Albert, 91
Rhatigan, Seamus, 195
Robinson, Mary, 77, 193
Roche, James, 137–8
Roche, William, 134
Russell, Ted, 125
Ryan, P.J., 136–7

Services, Industrial, Professional
    and Technical Union (SIPTU),
    93
Scott, Brendan, 24
Siege of Limerick, 130, 139, 143
Shannon Airport, 100
Shinnors, John, 112
Sinn Féin, 94, 107
Smith, Raymond, 6
socialism, 11, 13, 20, 25, 56, 73,
    94, 97, 117, 153

Socialist Party, 55
Socialists against Nationalism,
    29, 55–6
South, Seán, 125
Southill Association, 106
Spring, Dick, 21, 48, 50, 66, 70–1,
    78–88, 145, 193, 195
St Mary's Cathedral, 148
Steinbeck, John, 11
Stone Mad, 11
stonemasons' craft union, 150–1,
    154–6

Tait, Peter, 142
Thomas, Dylan, 195
Thornley, David, 21
Trade Disputes Act, 1946, 155
trade unions, xi, 7, 10, 12, 13, 16,
    19, 29, 32, 52, 57, 61, 84, 90, 93,
    94,110, 117, 122–4, 131, 144, 146,
    150–89, 191, 195
    history of, 151–3
Tressel, Robert, 12
Troy, Mary, 5, 194
Tully, Jimmy, 77–8

University of Limerick, 75, 113,
    124

Vatican II, 31
Verling, Luke, 20
Wallace, Joe, 51, 85, 94, 116, 118,
    172–3
Workers Alliance for Democrat-
    ic Settlement of the Northern
    Ireland Conflict, 30
Workers Party, 44, 47, 58, 66

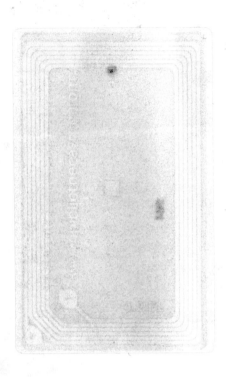